52 SIMPLE WAYS TO·BUILD FAMILY TRADITIONS

Paul Thigpen and Leisa Thigpen

OLIVER NELSON

Thomas Nelson Publishers
Nashville

To our parents

Bill Ghetti
Bonnie Ghetti
Travis Thigpen
Margaret Thigpen

and our children

Lydia Marie
Elijah John

Copyright © 1993 by Thomas Paul Thigpen

Published in Nashville, Tennessee, by Oliver-Nelson Books, a division of Thomas Nelson, Inc., Publishers, and distributed in Canada by Word Communications, Ltd., Richmond, British Columbia.

The Bible version used in this publication is THE NEW KING JAMES VERSION. Copyright © 1979, 1980, 1982, Thomas Nelson, Inc., Publishers.

Printed in the United States of America.

Library of Congress Cataloging-in-Publication Data

Thigpen, Thomas Paul, 1954-
    52 ways to build family traditions / Paul Thigpen and Leisa Thigpen.
        p.   cm.
    ISBN 0-8407-9673-0 (pbk.)
    1. Family festivals–United States.   2. Holidays–United States.
    3. United States–Social life and customs.   I. Thigpen, Leisa, 1956-   . II. Title. III. Title: Fifty-two ways to build family traditions.
GT2402.U6T48   1993
394.2–dc20   93-24920
                                                         CIP

3   4   5   6   —   98   97   96   95

Contents

Traditions for Special Times of the Day and
Week

Traditions for Family Milestones

Traditions for Celebrating Your Family Heritage

Traditions for Celebrating Family Achievements

Traditions for Building a Family Jargon

Traditions for Honoring and Serving One
Another

■ Introduction

Somewhere between the last bite of the corn bread dressing and the first bite of the pecan pie—that's when a basket is passed around each year at our family's Thanksgiving meal.

No, we aren't asking the kids for donations from their allowance to help pay for the turkey. Nor are we offering an extra round of homemade rolls for the guests. Instead, we ask everyone present to drop in the basket one at a time the three small kernels of dried corn that we've placed beside each dinner plate. With each kernel, we have them give at least one reason why they're thankful.

It's a small holiday habit, yet we never cease to be deeply moved by the results. Most often each speaker thanks God for someone else present while misty eyes around the table begin to glimmer in the candlelight. And when the guests go home in the evening, they invariably comment, "I want to do that again next year."

This simple practice requires almost no preparation or expense. But its rewards continue long after the meal is over, rippling out from our table into other homes as well. Such is the power and blessing of a meaningful family tradition.

Empty Rituals   In some circles, of course, *tradition* is a bad word. It too often refers to empty rituals or wooden habits whose meaning has long been forgotten. We're reminded, for example, of another family's Thanksgiving tradition in a home where ham, rather than turkey, was the holiday centerpiece. As the mother was preparing the ham for the oven one Thanksgiving morning, she told her daughter, "Now don't forget—before you bake the ham, always cut it in half and place it in two pans."

"Why?" asked the daughter.

"Oh, I'm not sure," said the mother, "but I've always done it that way because your grandmother always did it that way. She's in the living room—why don't you ask her?"

When the little girl asked, Grandma could only respond with the observation that her own mother had always done it that way too. So when Great-Grandma came into the room, the question was repeated once more.

"Why did you always cut the Thanksgiving ham in half before you baked it?" asked the little girl.

The elderly matriarch grinned. "Simple," she said. "We never had a pan big enough to hold the whole thing!"

No doubt some family traditions like this one can be empty habits rather than meaningful events. After all, according to the word's root meaning, a *tradition* is simply "something handed down"—and it's possible to hand down both burdens and blessings. But we believe that the biblical glimpses of family life in ancient Israel reflect God's desire that we strengthen our families with meaningful customs.

Meaningful Customs When the Israelites left Egypt to become a new nation, God commanded their families to hold special observances in their homes so that they would remember what He had done for them. Perhaps the best-known of these family traditions are the yearly Passover celebration (see Ex. 12:1–20) and the weekly Sabbath observance (see Ex. 20:8–11). Other significant Israelite family customs included circumcision (see Gen. 17:9–14), the Feast of Weeks and the Feast of Tabernacles (see Deut. 16:9–17).

These family traditions have endured in the Jewish community over thousands of years, accumulating countless embellishments. We've visited several Jewish homes at Passover, and we admit that in some families the festival customs have become empty. But in other homes where such customs are living reminders of spiritual realities, these traditions have strengthened families in many ways.

You can enrich your home life in a similar way by cultivating customs that reflect your family's unique personality and values. The resulting benefits—enhanced family identity, closeness, unity, and stability, among others—will reward your efforts both now and for years to come.

1 ■ Talk Over the Benefits of Family Traditions

No married couple who remember well their first Christmas as a family will doubt the importance of family traditions. The most sensitive conflict for many young couples in their first year of marriage is not over money or romance but over the celebration of Christmas.

Will gifts be opened on Christmas morning or Christmas Eve? Will the tree be real or artificial? Will we use plastic tinsel or hand-strung popcorn? Will Christmas dinner feature turkey or ham? Each spouse has an emotional investment in maintaining his or her own traditions, and the sparks may fly because family customs mean more to us than we realize.

But why exactly do they mean so much? What are the benefits of meaningful family traditions? Social research and practical experience suggest that the families with the strongest ties tend to have the most traditions because such traditions create and reinforce emotional security in the home.

Consider the Benefits As a first step in cultivating special customs in your home, find an evening or a weekend afternoon when every family member can be present for a family meeting. At the appointed time, make their favorite snack, find a comfortable place to relax together, and tell them what you want to do. Then talk over some specific benefits of family traditions. See if anyone can give an example of a custom you already have to illustrate each of the following points:

Traditions establish family continuity. When something is done again and again and through generations, it ties together past and present. It links year to year, childhood to adulthood, and grandparent to grandchild with shared experiences, values, and memories.

Traditions build family stability.   Consistent family customs provide regular, familiar patterns for a rhythm of life together. Whether it's bedtime stories every night or family games every Sunday afternoon, such customs add an element of predictability to family life that's both comfortable and comforting. This is especially important in a day when most families keep hectic, sometimes erratic schedules.

Traditions cultivate family identity.   Customs that help make a family unique can give its members a sense of who they are and where they belong. This quality is critical as a counterbalance to the intense pressure on today's youth to identify with their peers instead of with their families.

Traditions enrich family unity. Who can forget the warm sense of togetherness that comes when a family gathers for a Christmas morning gift-opening or a Fourth of July reunion? Meaningful customs build a sense of closeness that endures long after children have grown and distance separates family members.

Traditions reveal the significance of our lives. When we set aside the everyday routine for special customs, we focus on what's important to us. All too easily our days can slip by unnoticed until years have passed before we know it. Observing special days and events gives us a chance to pause and reflect on our lives.

Traditions symbolize how family members feel about one another. Family customs are much more than simple words or acts. They give those who take part in them a chance to say nonverbally, "I love you. I enjoy being with you. You are important, and what we share with each other is important."

In all these ways, meaningful family traditions make a family strong.

Talking together about the benefits of customs in your home will help your family understand why it's important to cultivate them, and it can get them excited about exploring some new ones.

2 ■ Take an Inventory of Your Family Traditions

We were arriving home after a long out-of-state trip. The whole family seemed happier than usual to be getting back to familiar surroundings, and as we turned the corner onto the street where we live, someone began singing a little song that begins, "Here we are all together as we sing our song joyfully . . ." The rest of us quickly joined in, and we finished the last bar just as we pulled into our driveway.

Months later, as we turned onto our street at the end of another long journey, you can guess what happened: the song broke out again, and we sang it with more gusto than ever. A new family tradition was born—a custom that today still expresses the delight we share in having a special place we call our own.

Like this one, some family customs are born spontaneously. Do something once, and it just seems so "right" that you do it again and again. Other family traditions are more like habits that grow gradually over a period of time, such as a particular strategy for decorating the tree at Christmas.

Existing Family Traditions   These kinds of customs tend to thrive naturally on their own. But others must be intentionally cultivated in order to survive. To help them grow, take an inventory of your current family traditions. Have your family answer the following questions:

Which of our family traditions have been carried on from the generations before us?   This question encourages your family to recognize its roots. It can also enhance your connections with grandparents and other older relatives as you ask them the reasons for your family traditions. For example, the family reunion you attend every summer may be an annual custom dating back several generations.

Which traditions are new to our family, and how did they develop?   Your children may not know why you've chosen to do things the way you do, so the special meaning of certain customs may be lost on them. They may even think that all families do things the same way and thus miss a chance to feel a sense of family identity and uniqueness.

Talking about the creation of traditions also gives you an opportunity to share family anecdotes with your children that provide them with new insights into their family history.

What do our family traditions mean to us? Why are they worth maintaining?   You may be surprised to find that the same custom has different meanings for different family members. You may also find that a tradition you thought relatively unimportant

—such as dyeing and hunting eggs on Easter weekend—is much more important to the children than to you.

Have any of our traditions lost their meaning? Why? Should we revitalize them, discontinue them, or replace them?   Like any ritual, a family tradition can become a lifeless routine if we don't continue to invest it with meaning. Some customs should be allowed to die. But that doesn't mean you should drop a tradition the first time it feels a little stale. Sometimes you can bring freshness to an old custom by discussing its significance or varying the details.

Have we lost any traditions that we would like to reestablish?   Perhaps sickness, a tight budget, or another unforeseen circumstance caused you to neglect a tradition once, and you never started it up again. Did you let it lapse because you didn't find it as meaningful as you'd hoped it would be? Or would it be worth another try?

Which new traditions would we like to begin?   This last question will take you to the next step in the process of building your family's traditions: holding a family tradition scavenger hunt. In the following chapters and in countless other places, you'll discover scores of ideas for adding to the collection of traditions in your home.

3 ■ Hold a Family Tradition Scavenger Hunt

Once your inventory has identified and evaluated your family's current traditions, you're ready to go looking for some new ones to enrich your home life. Why not have a scavenger hunt in which every family member looks for new customs to consider adopting?

Look for Ideas Ideas for new traditions can come from many sources. Consider the following scavenger hunt strategies:

Send one family member to talk to grandparents and other older relatives. Ask them to recall traditions they inherited from their parents or developed themselves. Find out which traditions were most meaningful and why. If a child takes this assignment, help him or her prepare "interview" questions, record the conversations on cassette, and replay your relatives' insights for the whole family to hear.

Have another family member interview other families about the traditions they observe. Ask the same questions and tape the responses for your family's later evaluation. Talk to neighbors, friends from church and school, even strangers in the local shopping mall!

Yet another family member can head for a bookstore and the public library. Look through books about

- marriage and family life, especially "how to" books with practical suggestions for fun and meaningful family activities.

- special seasons and holidays.

- the customs of earlier generations, such as a history book about how families lived in early America.

- traditions from Jewish culture, many of which are rooted in the Bible and can add a beautiful dimension to your family's spiritual life.

- customs in other lands, especially those countries that were home to your family's ancestors (see more about this subject in chapter 30).

At the same time, don't forget that magazines and newsletters focusing on family issues or Christian living may also provide ideas. Check children's magazines as well.

Finally, glean ideas from the following chapters in this book. Though not every idea provided here will work for you, these suggestions from our home and others have been tested and found to make a valuable contribution to the family tradition treasury.

Compile Suggestions   Once each family member has gathered ideas from his or her particular source, set aside an evening to compile the suggestions. You may want to categorize them according to the headings we have used for this book.

• Seasonal traditions

• Traditions for special times of the day and week

• Traditions for family milestones

• Traditions for celebrating your family heritage

• Traditions for celebrating family achievements

• Traditions for building a family jargon

• Traditions for honoring and serving one another

Take as long as you need to examine the merits of each custom and how it might be adapted to fit your unique circumstances. Give everyone a chance to comment and express approval or disapproval.

Don't force the issue if family members are strongly opposed to a particular idea. If someone is simply a little hesitant, however, you can offer to give the custom a try before making a final decision.

A word of caution: don't attempt to initiate too many new traditions at once. Add one or two at a time, giving your family a chance to get accustomed to them before you try more. The idea is to build up a comfortable, familiar rhythm of traditions—not to overwhelm your loved ones with changes.

When you've come up with an initial list of ideas you think will be right for your home, take a look at the last chapter of this book for help in applying what you've learned to make your family closer and stronger.

4 ■ Start the New Year Right

The year's first holiday, New Year's Day, arrives in many communities with fireworks and bonfires. Laws in many places don't allow private activities of that sort because of the fire hazard, so if you enjoy the lights and noise, make it a tradition to take part in the public events planned for your area.

Your Own Celebration   In addition, consider these New Year's customs:

Throw a New Year's Eve party with old family friends.   Make it a celebration for adults and children alike. New Year's Eve is a good time for looking back as well as looking forward; so to spark some good memories, invite guests to bring along photos, or perhaps a home video, that include someone from your family having fun with theirs. Or bring baby pictures, shuffle them, and see who can correctly identify the most baby faces. End the evening with a hearty rendition of "Auld Lang Syne."

Plan family goals and schedules for the new year. Make it a tradition to set some exciting yet realistic objectives, for each family member and for the family as a whole, to be accomplished in the next twelve months. Goals can be spiritual, physical, financial, or intellectual, or they can deal with any other important area of personal and family life.

Serve a special New Year's Day dinner. We serve a menu traditional to the South: black-eyed peas, ham hock, and rice. "Hoppin' John," as it's called, is an old favorite of many families in the South who have eaten it for "good luck" on New Year's Day for a number of generations. Check with older relatives in your family to find out if there's a traditional New Year's dish for your region or ethnic community.

Keep a New Year's journal that records the highlights of the year just past and mentions your hopes for the year to come. Talk over with the family the events that merit inclusion in such a family chronicle. You might let each family member write his or her own contribution to the book.

Start the new year with some new traditions—and develop a new sense of direction for the months ahead.

5 ∎ Show Your Love on Valentine's Day

Valentine's Day is a ready-made occasion for strengthening family relationships. Set aside some time to celebrate your affection and appreciation for one another.

Valentine's Day Traditions   Celebrate Valentine's Day with one or more of these expressions of love:

Make family valentines by hand.   Busy schedules may allow for only simple creations, but we believe that homemade cards are best whenever possible. Our most memorable creations end up in the family scrapbook.

Serve a Valentine's Day breakfast.   Make it a festive tradition, with toast cut into heart shapes and spread with strawberry jelly, flowers on the table, and whatever else your imagination creates to say to the family, "I love you."

Have family members create their own valentine mailboxes and decorate them to suit their fancies. Let each person deliver a valentine to each of the other boxes; then have a "mail call" at breakfast.

Think of ways to complete the sentence "I love you because . . ." for each family member. Write the completed sentence on a slip of paper and drop it in the valentine mailbox of the person described. Youngsters who can't yet write can dictate their sentiments to another family member.

The notes take only a few minutes to prepare, but the results can be deeply affirming. You may even be surprised at the things your family loves most about you!

Individualize the valentine tradition of sending flowers. You can freshen up this almost universal custom by choosing your own "trademark" flower to present every year rather than the standard red roses—perhaps peppermint carnations or a splashy bunch of golden mums. Or leave the flowers to be discovered in the same unusual place each year as your "signature." Leave a single yellow rose on a bed pillow . . . on the carseat . . . in the medicine cabinet!

With a little imagination, the unusual can become the traditional in your family's celebration of Valentine's Day.

6 ■ Deepen Your Family Spiritual Life During Lent

One of the oldest traditions in the Christian community is the observance of Lent. This season, beginning with the Wednesday of the seventh week before Easter and ending with Easter itself, has provided many generations of believers with a chance to deepen their spiritual lives through prayer, self-examination, and small acts of self-sacrifice.

At the heart of Lent is the custom of fasting—that is, of voluntarily giving up some kind of food or drink as a way of exercising self-discipline and concentrating on spiritual matters. Since Sunday is considered a day of celebration, Sundays are exempt from the fast. But the remaining forty days, recalling Jesus' forty-day fast in the wilderness, offer us a time to give something to God as a token of our love.

Guidelines for Fasting In our family, the Lenten sacrifice varies from person to person and from year to year. Sometimes we give up favorite foods, sometimes pleasurable activities. As your family observes Lent, take into consideration several factors as you decide how to fast, and talk them over as a family:

Give up something you genuinely value—perhaps a dessert, a favorite beverage, or a cherished pastime. Otherwise, the sacrifice has no meaning. Our daughter once slyly decided to give up broccoli, but we insisted she make another choice because going without that vegetable would have been for her a treat!

The sacrifice should be reasonable rather than extreme. In a zealous moment, our daughter once decided she would give up all sweets for Lent. But we knew that an eight-year-old girl would later be sorely tempted to break her commitment, so we suggested the alternative of giving up only candy. That was a promise she could more easily keep, and yet it was still a meaningful sacrifice.

Give up something that you're better off avoiding. Sweets, soft drinks, and coffee are foods that would fall into that category; television viewing is a healthy choice as an activity to give up for Lent.

Closer to God The discipline of self-sacrifice is only part of the Lenten tradition. We set aside this season to bring us closer to God and to make us more like Him, so we should take on positive things as well as give up others. For that reason, we make it a custom to spend extra time in regular prayer during the days of Lent, talking with God especially about the ways we need to change our lives. We also attend Lenten church services when we can.

One natural way we focus on positive acts of devotion is to dedicate to godly purposes whatever time or money we save from the things we give up. If we "fast" television viewing, for example, the extra time on our hands would be well spent reading Scripture, praying, keeping a spiritual journal, or helping others. We can collect money normally spent on dessert or soft drinks in a jar on the family dining table and give it to someone in need at the end of the season.

Despite the subdued atmosphere of Lent, with its focus on repentance and its foregoing of pleasures, this tradition can bring your family a renewed sense of peace. By consciously cultivating spiritual growth during these weeks, you can rediscover right priorities, and the Easter celebration will be more festive than ever.

7 ■ Celebrate the Resurrection on Easter

Ever since that glorious Sunday morning when Jesus rose from the grave, the church has commemorated this greatest event in its history with an annual celebration. Most families observe the day by joining with other believers in joyous worship services—including the traditional sunrise service, often held outdoors.

Less obviously "spiritual" but just as festive is the custom of dyeing and hunting eggs. Some parents, of course, dislike the "eggs and rabbits" theme for Easter, feeling that it turns attention away from the true significance of the day. Our family, too, avoids talk of an Easter bunny, but because the egg is a traditional symbol of new life, we think it's an appropriate element in Easter celebrations.

Make Easter Special   Borrow a few customs from our home to emphasize the significance of Easter:

Observe Palm Sunday with a family skit reenacting Jesus' triumphal entry into Jerusalem. At our house, we read aloud the scriptural account of the first Palm Sunday in Matthew 21:1–11. Then each family member takes a turn playing the role of Jesus. He or she rides a donkey (actually a stick horse) throughout the house, while the rest of us sing praise choruses and wave palm branches and articles of clothing.

Establish a week-long Holy Week tradition using an Easter egg tree.   Several years ago we set a small, multi-branched tree limb upright in a bucket of plaster of paris and painted it white. Each year we decorate it with colorful bows and ornaments, such as eggs and butterflies, that symbolize new life and resurrection.

Eight of the eggs we place on the tree are hollow plastic shells numbered 1 through 8. Inside each of these is a passage of Scripture to be read for each of the eight days of Holy Week, beginning with Palm Sunday.

- Palm Sunday: Matthew 21:1–11

- Monday: Matthew 21:12–17

- Tuesday: Matthew 21:18–22

- Wednesday: Matthew 26:6–13

- Maundy Thursday: Matthew 26:17–30

- Good Friday: Matthew 27:27–54

- Holy Saturday: Matthew 27:55–66

- Easter Sunday: Matthew 28:1–20

Decorate eggs with spiritual themes. Bible verses, crosses, doves, or symbols of new life like the Easter lily or the butterfly are examples.

Make Easter baskets for your children that include items with a spiritual focus:

- a Bible-verse bookmark
- a small book on some spiritual subject
- a cassette of praise music
- fresh wildflowers
- a small amount of candy to break their Lenten fast.

Choose one or more families in your neighborhood to receive a surprise Easter basket. The ones we make are small—often crafted from pint-size strawberry baskets—but we fill them up with personalized eggs and the same kinds of treats we put in our children's baskets. The surprise baskets are left on our friends' front doorsteps early on Easter morning.

Hang a large painted banner that proclaims "He Is Risen!" across the front of your home. Do this late Saturday night so that it greets your neighbors first thing Easter morning.

We're careful to invest all our Easter traditions, even egg dyeing, with spiritual significance. That way we can make sure our children are aware of this most important of all Christian holidays.

8 ∎ Enjoy a Passover Seder

For many generations the Jewish people have celebrated God's faithfulness through the tradition of the Passover *seder*—a special meal commemorating their ancestors' escape from slavery in Egypt.

Our first encounter with a seder came when Jewish friends invited Paul (he was still single then) to join them for the feast. He was deeply moved by the rich symbolism of the ritual, the beauty of the liturgy, and the warmth of the family atmosphere. At first Paul felt envious of the tradition, but then he realized that as "adopted" children of Abraham, Christians too can claim the Exodus as part of their spiritual history (see Romans 9:8). So he obtained a copy of the order of service for the celebration (called the *haggadah*) and studied its ritual. Then, several years later, he led a seder for our family.

Our Passover Celebration We invited friends to join us, and the result was an evening we'll never forget. As far as possible we followed all the traditional rules for food preparation, table setting, and ritual, though the order of service itself varies among different Jewish communities.

The meaning of each custom was explained as we observed it, so by the end of the evening we all felt as if we'd had a short course in history and theology.

Since that first seder, we've celebrated Passover in both small and large settings—once with several hundred people participating. But the result has always been a memorable and educational celebration of God's faithfulness.

Resources Over the years, we've developed our own haggadah, tailored to our family's needs and interests. But if you're just starting out with this family tradition, we recommend that you check your public library for resources to help you plan and carry out the event. For an order of service that brings out beautifully the Passover's foreshadowing of our salvation through Jesus, we recommend *Passover Haggadah: A Messianic Celebration,* arranged by Eric-Peter Lipton (San Francisco: Jews for Jesus Publishing, 1986). Some supermarkets also distribute free of charge a more traditional haggadah, compliments of the people who make Maxwell House coffee.

Whichever order of service you use, you're sure to find that in the Passover tradition your family will commemorate one of the most important events in our spiritual history.

9 ▪ Honor Parents on Mother's Day and Father's Day

Just in case American families needed an annual reminder to honor their mothers, a new national tradition was born in 1908 when the second Sunday in May was declared Mother's Day. To keep Dad from being left out, the third Sunday in June was made Father's Day in 1927.

Honoring Mom and Dad   In our home, we treat these days with much the same fanfare as birthdays. Consider these ideas for making Mom or Dad feel special:

Exempt the honored parent from all household responsibilities for the day.   Chores that can wait until another day are postponed. Responsibilities that can't wait are delegated to the other parent or to an older child.

Create a centerpiece for your dining table that celebrates Mom or Dad.   Have each of the other family members contribute some item that symbolizes his or her appreciation for the honoree's special role in the family. Arrange snapshots, cooking utensils, a garden spade, garden flowers, car keys, a calculator—whatever seems appropriate—as a table decoration, and add a homemade card that expresses your love.

In addition to the typical gift of perfume or a necktie, give love coupons. Create a booklet of homemade coupons, each one entitling Mom or Dad to some small service and redeemable at a time he or she chooses. Coupons could offer these services:

- A ten-minute back rub

- A Saturday afternoon out window shopping alone

- An evening without having to cook dinner

- A Sunday afternoon nap without disturbance

- A one-time exemption from a weekly chore of the receiver's choice.

Adopt an extra mother or father for the day. Have your family choose someone who's a parent but doesn't have children living nearby, or someone without children who's been like a parent to your kids, and invite that person over to share the day with you. Treat him or her with the same gifts and honors you give to the mom or dad in your home.

Any of these traditions will remind the moms and dads in your world that they are unique and irreplaceable—and that's what these special Sundays are for.

10 ■ Honor Your Country on Independence Day

Fourth of July traditions represent for many of us the most memorable of summertime activities: parades, picnics, fireworks, patriotic rallies, and neighborhood cookouts. Because Independence Day is a tradition all Americans can share in, regardless of their spiritual background, this particular holiday holds the potential for drawing us closer to our neighbors and to our community as a whole.

Private Observances   In addition to public Independence Day traditions, your family may want to cultivate some private customs. Here are a few ideas:

Throw a block party for the holiday.   Have each family bring a covered dish so that no one home bears too much of the burden of preparation. Our neighborhood celebration climaxes when the family down the street fires their antique cannon, a tradition they observe on New Year's Eve as well.

Write a family letter to your senator, your congressman, or even the President.   Tell him or her of your concerns and your positions on various issues facing the country. Then spend a few minutes praying for them and for the national concerns you've written about. This custom will signal to your children the importance of interceding for government officials and expressing opinions to them. Mail letters to these addresses:

- For the President:
  The White House
  1600 Pennsylvania Avenue, NW
  Washington, DC 20500

- For any member of the U.S. House of Representatives:
  Representative [Name]
  House Office Building
  Washington, DC 20515

- For any U.S. Senator:
  Senator [Name]
  Senate Office Building
  Washington, DC 20510

Hold your own family rally. Pledge the flag, sing patriotic songs, and present a skit about some event in our nation's history. Or read together a poem such as one of these:

- "Columbus" by Joaquin Miller

- "The Landing of the Pilgrim Fathers in New England" by Felicia Dorothea Hemans

- "Paul Revere's Ride" by Henry Wadsworth Longfellow
- "Concord Hymn" by Ralph Waldo Emerson
- "Old Glory" by James Whitcomb Riley

Have an old-fashioned picnic with traditional American foods. Churn homemade ice cream. Drink hand-squeezed lemonade. Eat watermelon to your heart's content—then have a seed spitting contest to see who can propel them the farthest! Try a three-legged race or a potato sack race. Use red, white and blue paper goods to remind you why you're celebrating.

11 ■ Create Yearly Vacation Traditions

The two-week annual vacation has become an established rite for many American families. Some find a favorite spot and return there year after year at the same time—perhaps a cottage on the beach in July or a cabin in the mountains in October. Such a familiar "home away from home" becomes part of the family tradition—a comfortable, stable element in their annual calendar that, like Christmas or Thanksgiving, accumulates fond memories over the years.

Other families are more adventurous. They love to visit a different place each year to see new sights and tackle new challenges. They have fun exploring the surprises along the road to their destination and may even change all their plans if something they find there looks intriguing. For them, the search for adventure is itself the custom.

Your Vacation Tradition Whichever style is yours, you can enrich your family getaway tradition in several ways:

Liven up travel time with songs and games. Over the years, we've developed a standard repertoire of lighthearted choruses like "Old Susanna," "Polly-Wolly-Doodle," and "I Know an Old Lady Who Swallowed a Fly" that make the time fly. We've also collected a number of games every family member can play in the car, such as "I Spy," "Boticelli," "Hinky-Pinky," and a few of our own creation. No long-distance trip seems complete to us without singing and playing as we head down the road.

Schedule a traditional vacation event. Whether or not you get away to the same spot every year, you can create a sense of continuity by building into the vacation schedule a traditional activity. One family we know gets dressed up the last evening of every vacation, wherever they are, and eats at a fancy restaurant. Another family makes sure that they take an hour or two at the end of the trip to review their favorite moments from the previous few days and to talk about what they would do differently the next time. Other families make it a point every year to take a long morning walk together, stay up for a late-night talk around a fire, or battle it out in an old-fashioned pillow fight!

Have vacation rules. In one family we know, family members are forbidden to take along on vacation any watches or clocks; that way the pace is sure to be relaxed. Another family guarantees a casual getaway by outlawing dress clothes and razors for the trip.

Weekend Trips Consider making it a family custom to get away regularly for weekend trips in addition to your annual vacation. Here are some ideas for "mini" getaways you could repeat every year:

A back roads vacation. Tour the countryside without traveling on any freeways, interstate highways, or city streets. Keep a family journal of what you see.

A kid-planned vacation. Have children make all the decisions about destination, meals, lodging, and activities. Parents can establish a budget and reserve the right to approve the final plan.

An educational vacation. Visit a museum, historical sight, factory, or farm. Learn how to milk a cow, pan for gold, or make a quilt.

A service vacation. Tackle a service project away from home that your family can accomplish together. Work at a homeless shelter, help an elderly couple repair their home, or collect door-to-door for your favorite charity.

12 ■ Replace Halloween with All Saints' Day

Most of the American children in our generation took part in Halloween, and we were no exception. We painted our faces, donned our costumes, and went door-to-door collecting enough treats to last us a month. The fun seemed innocent enough.

Sadly, the holiday has degenerated since the days when we were young, reflecting the decline in our culture as well. Costumes are often gruesome, celebrating violence with masks of characters from slasher films. Others reflect occult practices, identifying with the ceremonies of neo-pagan witches and satanists who hold Halloween in high esteem. Meanwhile, pranks have escalated into serious crimes of vandalism, arson, and physical assault, and the children themselves sometimes become victims of poisoned treats or even kidnapping. Halloween has become an annual occasion for glorifying evil.

All Saints' Day   Ironically, Halloween is a corruption of an ancient Christian celebration, All Saints' Day. The festival dates back to the early Middle Ages in Europe, when Christians set aside a day (and the evening before) to honor the heroes of the faith.

We've concluded that the best way to treat Halloween is replace it with activities that recapture this tradition of remembering great men and women of God. For that reason, we make it our custom to take part in one of the Halloween alternative celebrations, such as the harvest festivals or "Hallelujah Night" parties held by many churches today. When we attend these festivities, our family members, parents included, usually dress up as heroic biblical characters or figures from church history.

Going out for the evening means that we aren't around to hand out candy to trick-or-treaters. Neighborhood children may be disappointed that we aren't home when they come around that night, but we think it's best not to encourage Halloween customs in any way.

Many Christians disagree with our approach to Halloween. Some feel obligated to treat the children who come to their door and may even give out gospel tracts with the candy. Others think that the fun is still innocent enough. Still others insist that the occasion should be ignored altogether.

Each family must follow its own convictions. But our experience has shown that the tradition of celebrating a true All Saints' Day turns our attention to God's faithfulness through the ages and provides us with role models worthy of our imitation.

13 ■ Make Thanksgiving a Day of Gratitude

Thanksgiving celebrations rank high on the list of family traditions because in most American homes, the occasion is second only to Christmas as a time for family. Thanksgiving also stands apart as a holiday dedicated not to honoring a hero or commemorating a past event but rather to cultivating an attitude of the heart. If we spend the day only in feasting and football, we miss the whole point.

Focus on Gratitude That doesn't mean we shouldn't spread the table with good food or cheer our favorite teams on the gridiron. But we can keep those happy Thanksgiving customs while maintaining—or for some of us, regaining—the spiritual focus of the day. Here are some suggestions:

Make prayer a high point of the family gathering. The table grace said before the big meal easily provides a focal point for our thanks to God. In some families, the tradition is to have the oldest person present bless the food; in others, it's the youngest who does so.

Read a passage of Scripture.   Our family usually reads one of the Psalms that express gratitude just before we bless the meal. Consider reading Psalm 100 or Psalm 136 at your holiday table.

Sing traditional songs associated with Thanksgiving, such as the hymns "We Gather Together," "We Plow the Fields," and "Come Ye Thankful People, Come."

Adopt the Thanksgiving tradition we described in the introduction.   Pass around a small basket at the Thanksgiving table. Have each person present drop three kernels of dried corn in the basket, one at a time, while naming three things he or she is thankful for.

Share your family's abundance with those in need. Consider these activities:

- Present a generous financial gift each November to an organization that feeds hungry people.

- Invite to Thanksgiving dinner someone who otherwise would be alone this day.

- Volunteer at a local soup kitchen that feeds the homeless.

14 ■ Prepare the Way of the Lord Through Advent

The church calendar begins with Advent, a time of spiritual preparation for Christmas. Advent—which literally means "the coming"—focuses our attention on the two comings of Christ: the first one as Savior nearly two thousand years ago, the second one as Judge when history will come to an end.

Advent Traditions   The season begins on the fourth Sunday before Christmas. From then until Christmas Eve, Christians around the world join to turn their hearts toward Jesus in gratitude for His earthly life. Here's how our family observes this special time:

An Advent calendar   Years ago we created an Advent calendar, much like the ones available commercially but with a unique feature: the pictures behind the flaps are accompanied by verses of Scripture, each one connecting the picture to the life of Jesus. For example, a picture of a lamb has the reference John 1:29, which tells about the Lamb of God; a picture of a flame has Matthew

3:11, which says that Jesus would baptize in the Holy Spirit and fire.

Each night after dinner, we open the calendar flap for that day and read the verse noted behind it. Then we talk about the meaning of the verse and sing a Christmas carol.

An Advent wreath   We also light the candles of an Advent wreath. You can purchase a wreath made of evergreens and fitted with four candles, or you can make one yourself. Traditionally, three of the candles are purple and one is pink. We like to add a large white candle in the middle, called the Christ candle.

We follow the customary ritual: on the first Sunday in Advent and every evening of the following week, we light one purple candle. During the second week, we light two candles; the third Sunday, three (this is when the pink candle is first lit); and the fourth, all four. On Christmas Eve, we light the Christ candle as well.

We keep the candles lit each evening as we open the calendar door, read and discuss the scriptural text for the day, and sing. On Christmas Eve, we light additional candles throughout the house and keep them burning all evening until bedtime.

The Christmas tree   Our Christmas tree usually goes up on the first Sunday in Advent so we can enjoy it the whole season. We make the evening of tree trimming an important occasion in itself by surrounding it with small traditions:

- Each child receives that evening an inexpensive "Happy Advent" gift—often an ornament they can use for the season.

- The family receives a new cassette tape of Christmas music to keep our seasonal collection expanding.

- While we trim the tree we listen to Christmas music and drink hot cocoa (unless the Florida weather is just too hot).

A new tradition.   This year we want to establish a new tradition: Christmas card prayers. During Advent, we hang the cards we receive along the kitchen counter to enjoy them. This December, we plan to select a card or two each evening before we pray over our dinner. We'll include the senders in our prayer. It's a good way to keep close to our hearts the loved ones who are far away.

With these and other Advent customs, your family can fulfill the words of the old Christmas carol: "Let every heart prepare Him room."

15 ■ Make Christmas the Most Memorable Celebration of All

In many homes, Christmas is synonymous with family traditions. Even families without special customs the rest of the year usually find themselves falling into the familiar rites of the season: tree trimming, home decorating, treat baking, gift giving, carol singing.

Additional Christmas Customs Whatever your family's Christmas habits, there's always room for a few more to enrich the celebration of Jesus' birth. Consider these:

Make your Christmas tree a family history book. Each year since we were married, we've crafted or purchased one ornament that symbolizes what we feel to be the most significant event of the year. Then we date it and give it a place of honor on the tree. We added a baby's alphabet block the year our daughter was born, a toy house the year we built our first home, a palm tree the year we moved to Florida. Each Christmas as we look at these ornaments, we remember together our unique family history, and we share the fond memories with our children.

Give each child his or her own tree ornament with the date engraved or painted on it. Someday, when your children move away and trim their own trees, they won't be starting from scratch, and the memories of your holidays together will go with them.

Revive the tradition of Christmas caroling. Carol through the neighborhood, then come back to the house for hot cocoa, apple cider, and cookies. Some of our fondest Christmas memories come from the moments we've spent singing "Silent Night" on a front doorstep, while little children gazed in delight at our flickering candles and their parents sang along with tears in their eyes.

Make a Christmas box for Jesus. One family we know does this every year. Each family member makes a Christmas card addressed to Jesus and places it in the box. On the cards they write: "Dear Jesus, I will give my love to You this Christmas by doing the following . . ." Then they fill in the blanks with deeds of kindness to be done during the Christmas season for someone specific.

After they put the cards in the box, they gift wrap it with a name tag for Jesus and place it under the tree with the other gifts. On Christmas morning they open the box and read the cards aloud, and each person tells how his or her "gift for Jesus" turned out.

Just for fun, pass around a gag gift year after year. Whoever receives it one year should wrap it and give it the next year to a different family member. But in order for the gift to be a surprise, the packaging must be misleading so that the person who receives it doesn't know what it is until it's opened.

Recycle your Christmas tree by giving it to the birds. After Christmas, remove all the ornaments but leave any popcorn or cranberries. Add a few crusts of bread hung from loops of string along with some muffin tin liners filled with birdseed. Pine cones stuffed with peanut butter and birdseed also make excellent feeders. Place the tree in your backyard and enjoy the days after Christmas watching your hungry little friends enjoy their own holiday feast!

With traditions like these, you can make Christmas the most memorable family celebration of all.

16 ■ Build a Habit of Family Devotions

Few traditions have the potential to touch our lives more deeply than a regular family devotional time. Yet few traditions are more difficult to maintain. In addition to the problem of hectic and irregular family schedules, we face the challenge of keeping our times with God fresh despite the need for some sort of routine.

Worth the Effort Admittedly, in our own home we haven't yet achieved the kind of consistency we want for this area of our life together. But we're convinced that some kind of regular family devotion is worth whatever labor is required to maintain it. As we continue to work at building this habit, we keep in mind some tips from families who are much further along than we are:

If you can't seem to carve out a daily time for family devotions, don't give up altogether; instead, do it once a week. If you can't find half an hour, find ten minutes. Something is better than nothing. Once you get going, you may discover that finding time wasn't the real problem after all; the tough part was building a habit. Once the habit is established, increasing the time and frequency may come more easily than you think.

Select together a place in your home where you'll regularly meet for devotions. A consistent location builds an important sense of familiarity and continuity. For freshness, pick an unusual place one out of every four or five times you meet. You may even want to designate a particular chair as the "prayer chair." Then, whenever someone in your family faces an important decision, crisis, or some other need, he or she can sit in the chair while the rest of you gather around and pray.

Don't let one person do it all. A basic agenda for family devotions is worship, Scripture reading, discussing what was read, and praying for family needs. Everyone can take part.

Family Prayer As you pray together, keep in mind these guidelines:

Lead by example. Allow your children to see and hear you pray often.

Build on your children's natural sense of wonder and appreciation. Encourage them to thank and praise God for the things they find awesome, beautiful or pleasurable.

Use traditional as well as spontaneous prayers. Small children especially need the continuity and familiarity of prayers they've memorized. But they also need to know that they can talk freely with God as they would with a family member or friend.

Allow children to be honest in prayer—even if it means telling God they're angry, sad, or afraid. Then encourage them to ask the Lord for help in overcoming their unwelcome thoughts, attitudes, and feelings.

Pray specifically instead of generally, so your family can recognize God's specific answers. One family we know has a tradition called "The Thanksgiving Book." Together they've kept a journal of the specific family prayers God has answered. The book cultivates gratitude as well as faith when they go to God in prayer.

Keep your devotions fresh by introducing variety into your devotions. Use skits or role playing to spark discussion. A regular family devotion doesn't have to be routine.

17 ■ Sing a Table Grace

One of the traditions enjoyed most by visitors to our home is our mealtime custom of singing a table grace. The song is followed by a short prayer of thanks—usually spoken by our youngest family member. Each day a different person gets to choose what we'll sing, and since we've been collecting songs for several years, by now we have quite a collection to choose from. If guests are present and aren't familiar with the song we choose, we either teach it to them (they're all simple) or let them choose another song.

Table Grace Ideas   If you'd like to make singing around your table a family tradition, here are a few ideas to get you going:

The Doxology   ("Praise God from whom all blessings flow . . .") We sing this choral response using several different melodies learned in various churches.

The Gloria Patri   ("Glory be to the Father . . .") We also sing various musical settings of this ancient song.

The Johnny Appleseed Blessing   Familiar to many from their childhood days in summer camp, we learned it from a family in an apple-growing area in southern California.

Praise choruses   "Thank You, Thank You, Jesus," "God, You're So Good," and "Bless the Lord, O My Soul" are especially fitting for giving thanks around the table.

You can make up your own table grace song. Use familiar tunes with a repetitive melody line, adding a few simple words. Sing to the tune of "Mary Had a Little Lamb":

"Oh, give thanks unto the Lord, to the Lord, to the Lord; Oh, give thanks unto the Lord, for all He's done for us." To the tune of "For He's a Jolly Good Fellow," sing "We bless the name of the Lord; we bless the name of the Lord; we bless the name of the Lord, for life and health and food."

There are many simple tunes you can adapt in this way. Whatever songs you choose as mealtime prayers, they're sure to enrich your time together. With a little imagination, you can build an entire repertoire of songs of praise to grace your family meals.

18 ■ Serve Food for Thought at Dinnertime

Studies undertaken to identify the traits of a strong family all agree on at least one point: the best home environments encourage healthy communication. When we consider that in many homes the evening meal provides the only occasion when the entire family comes together, we begin to see the importance of dinnertime conversation.

Conversation Strategies No doubt some topics—such as disciplinary issues—should be saved for another time and place because negative feelings hinder digestion. But that still leaves a host of subjects open to exploration. To build a tradition of healthy communication in your home, try these ideas to get your family talking around the table:

Discuss the day's news. Assign one or more children a "dinner news report" that summarizes the articles on the front page of the paper or the stories on the evening TV broadcast. As the report is given, ask lots of "why" questions about the basic causes, implications, moral issues, and historical significance of the events noted.

Play a game of Word Memories.   Have each child think of one word to give each parent. Then, respond with a true story from your past, especially your childhood, that's built around that word. For example, if the word is "bicycle," tell a story involving a bike.

Play Switcheroo, a game in which each family member must take another person's regular place at the dinner table.   Throughout the meal, act like the person whose place you've taken. If you have small children, you might want to warn them ahead of time so they can watch the people they'll have to imitate. Be ready for some laughter, surprises, and a healthy dose of honesty.

Play a game of Family Trivia.   See if your children can answer questions like these: In what year were Mom and Dad married? What were your grandmothers' maiden names? How many first cousins do you have? How old is Grandpa?

Become the Answer Man (or Woman).   Give each child permission to ask you one question. Anything goes, and if you don't know the answer, you must try to have it by dinnertime the next evening.

Give advance notice of a topic that you'd like to focus on at the dinner table the next evening.   That way you'll build a sense of expectancy, get everyone thinking about what they'll contribute, and give a useful focus to the conversation.

19 ■ Send Them to Bed with a Blessing

Bedtime is a reflective time for most children. They leave behind the busyness of the day and become especially open to what parents have to say. Early on we decided to take advantage of this teachable moment by cultivating nightly traditions that turn our children's attention toward God.

Bedtime Rituals First of all, we have each family member note at least one thing he or she is thankful for that has happened that day. This habit encourages gratitude, and it helps prompt discussion about what God is doing in our lives.

Next, we pray, both spontaneously and with traditional bedtime prayers such as the Lord's Prayer or the one that begins "Now I lay me down to sleep . . ." Then we sing a soft song of praise.

The Family Blessing All these customs, we're convinced, bless our kids, even as they bless us. But perhaps the most important tradition of the evening—one we began when our daughter was quite young—is the giving of an explicit *family blessing*.

In the Bible we find many examples of one person speaking a blessing on another, often accompanied by a gesture such as laying a hand on the head of the person receiving the blessing. In the Old Testament, patriarchs, priests, and prophets practiced this custom (see Gen. 14:18–20; 27:1–40; Num. 23:7–24:9). In the New Testament, Jesus laid His hands on the children and blessed them (see Mark 10:16).

In a similar way we speak a blessing on our children every night. The ritual is simple. One of us simply lays a hand on each one's head and says the words God gave the high priest Aaron for blessing the people:

> The LORD bless you and keep you;
> The LORD make His face shine upon you,
> And be gracious to you;
> The LORD lift up His countenance upon you,
> And give you peace.

We add, "In the name of the Father, and of the Son, and of the Holy Spirit. Amen."

It's as brief as that. But the benefits reaped by this particular family tradition are profound. Parents who bless their children this way accomplish several purposes:

A prayer of faith and authority   The blessing is actually a prayer of faith on behalf of the children. God's power is unleashed for their benefit when parents, standing in a God-ordained place of authority, speak the goodness of God to their children.

An affirmation of value A blessing affirms a child's worth and importance, saying in effect, "You are precious to me and to God. For this moment, I am giving my full attention to you and your welfare."

A sense of security A blessing assures children that their parents and their Heavenly Father love them and desire to protect and provide for them. It cultivates a feeling of safety and security—a feeling reinforced by laying hands on them. That sense of security helps prepare them to rest for the night.

Keep in mind that bedtime isn't the only time for a blessing; perhaps another part of the day would be best for your family's schedule. Remember as well that the biblical blessing we use is only one of many blessings possible.

The important thing is to bless your children, and to do it often. The rewards will last a lifetime.

20 ■ Make Sunday a Real Sabbath

Despite all the lip service given the Ten Commandments in Christian homes, the fourth commandment is all but forgotten by most: "Remember the Sabbath day, to keep it holy. . . . In it you shall do no work" (Ex. 20:8, 10). Sadly enough, many families typically spend Sunday catching up on chores that weren't taken care of during the previous week. Also, many people have jobs that require them to work through the weekend.

Of course, we don't want to be like the religious people Jesus reprimanded for making the Sabbath into a legalistic burden full of petty regulations (see Matt. 12:1–14). Nor do we want to insist as some Christians in earlier generations did that recreation should be outlawed on the Sabbath; having fun can certainly be an important part of getting rested and refreshed. Nevertheless, we've come to see that the principle of a regular Sabbath rest remains integral to God's plan for His creation (see Gen. 2:2–3). If the Lord Himself rested after His labors, shouldn't we do the same?

The traditional Jewish Sabbath is Saturday. The traditional Christian Sabbath is either that day or Sunday, because Jesus rose from the grave on Sunday. Whatever day fits best in a family's schedule, we believe it's important to set aside one day a week for rest.

The Family Sabbath Sometimes, of course, we have to labor to enter into rest. We may have to prepare ahead for the day—in fact, Friday was known to the ancient Jews as the "Day of Preparation" for that very reason. In our home, we do all we can to take care of necessary business on Saturday so that Sunday remains free for relaxation.

Once Sunday comes, we postpone chores until another day. The rule in our house is that no one cleans rooms, makes beds, or performs other household duties on Sunday. We eat leftovers on paper plates so that there is no food to prepare and no dishes to wash.

Some families we know like to begin their Sabbath at sunset on the evening before, as was the ancient Jewish custom. They light a candle as they sit down to the Saturday evening meal, and the candle remains lit until sunset on Sunday. They have other customs as well for this Sabbath dinner: a table grace sung only on that weekly occasion, a Sabbath blessing spoken by the parents to the children, and even a particular food prepared exclusively for the Sabbath.

However you choose to make the Sabbath a weekly tradition in your home, you'll find that the pause refreshes and strengthens you for your labors throughout the rest of the week.

21 ■ Create a Weekly Family Night

In the last few decades, the tradition of a weekly family night has been spreading throughout the Christian community in America. Some congregations even call a moratorium on church activities, one night a week to encourage families to stay at home for the evening.

The typical agenda for a family night is simple:

- Fun—singing, games, other pleasurable activities

- Feedback—sharing problems, needs, frustrations

- Focus—studying a biblical subject related to family needs and growth in skills and attitudes

- Prayer—remembering needs, concerns, and thanksgivings to God

- Coordination—planning the week's calendar, activities, and errands

Having Fun Because other chapters in this book overlap with the last four items of this agenda, we'd like to offer here a few ideas for having fun. In fact, some families prefer to focus their family night hours on the fun part and take care of the other items at a different time, perhaps at a weekly family council meeting (see chapter 22). For simple fun, try these activities together:

Ham Night On separate slips of paper, write the following phrases (or invent your own): jaywalkers; sixth-grade Sunday school class; people at a sale; commuters on a train; older couple out for a stroll; cars trying to get on the freeway at rush hour. Have each person draw a slip and act out the concept while the others try to guess what's being dramatized.

Note Night Distribute supplies for writing notes to five people chosen from among family members, friends you haven't seen in a while, missionaries, pastors, or teachers. You can each write to a different person or slip individual notes into an envelope for the same person.

Library Night Take the whole family to the public library and spend a few hours browsing the shelves together. Check out books each family member can enjoy, including one you can read together aloud over several evenings. You'll be better prepared for this venture if you keep a list of subjects that your children show an interest in during their daily conversations.

Reverse Roles Think of some typical family conflicts and act them out playing reversed roles—that is, have parents play the children and children play the parents.

Family Collage Choose any meaningful theme as the subject of a collage to be created on a large poster board. Supply each person with scissors, glue, and a collection of greeting cards, magazines, catalogs, and old snapshots. Each family member should be assigned an area of the board to work on alone. Compose the center together. Display the finished product in your home for a week or two.

How-To Night Have one family member teach the others a practical skill, such as how to change a tire, bake a pie, sew a button, or balance a checkbook.

Activities for family night are limited only by your imagination and a single rule: no one gets left out. With this weekly tradition, you're sure to make some lifelong memories.

22 ■ Hold a Weekly Family Council

One alternative to the weekly family night is the family council. Some families may be spending sufficient time playing together yet still feel the need to set aside time to conduct regular family business. If that's the case in your home, taking a few hours every week for a council meeting could strengthen your family life.

Planning Family Councils Choose a regular time to meet when all can be present and insist that everyone keep that time slot free.

The setting you choose is also important. Family members should meet facing one another, preferably around a table, without the distractions of TV, radio, stereo, or phone.

Family councils can accomplish a number of objectives:

- Identify family goals and priorities
- Target family weaknesses to improve and family strengths to affirm
- Resolve conflicts

- Plan events and coordinate schedules
- Arrange for maintenance functions such as chores and budgets
- Share family news

Council Rules   The family council is a good place for children to learn the skills of group decision making. They can contribute ideas and vote on issues that they're mature enough to consider. Be sure to lay ground rules for discussion like these:

- Everyone participates.
- Everyone gets a chance to talk about any matter of concern.
- Everyone listens and no one interrupts.
- Discussions must focus on finding solutions.
- Disagreement is all right if expressed respectfully.
- Agreements made at a meeting are in effect until the next meeting.

Keep the focus of the family council positive, include everyone, and before long your home will be running more smoothly than ever.

23 ▪ Welcome New Additions into the World

The common milestones of family life provide wonderful occasions for traditions—beginning with the arrival of a new child. Most Christian homes already observe at least a few birth customs, such as baby showers, baptism or dedication, birth announcements, and baby books.

New Traditions Consider a few other ideas that could make this occasion even more meaningful:

Start a new tradition by inviting the father and his male friends and relatives to a New Dad Shower. When we did this for our friend Terry, party guests participated in two ways.

First, we mailed with the invitations several questions about the guests' own experiences as fathers or sons. At the shower, they took turns answering queries like *What's the most important lesson you've ever learned from your own father or son? What qualities does Terry have that will make him a good father?*

Second, the men brought gifts that affirmed the specialness of the father-child relationship: "I Love

Daddy" bibs; "Dad" mugs; toys a father and child would enjoy playing with together, such as blocks or toy cars.

Write a letter to your unborn child.   Express the pleasure and excitement you feel as a parent. Talk about the kind of person you hope your child will become. Place the letter in a safe deposit box to be opened and read on the child's twelfth birthday.

Make naming your child a meaningful tradition. Take into account the meaning of the names you're considering. Several good books of names and their meanings are currently on the market.

Our custom is to list attractive biblical names for the new baby and study both their literal meanings and the lives of the people in Scripture who bore each name. We ask ourselves, "Would this biblical figure make a worthy role model for a child?"

After much prayer, we make our choice. Then we make sure that the name and its meaning are displayed prominently in the child's new surroundings, perhaps hanging a plaque on the nursery wall. As the child grows up, we remind him or her frequently of the significance of that name.

Some parents prefer to give family names according to a long-standing tradition among their relatives. Whatever your approach to naming children, remember that the names you give to them can serve as a tradition that connects them with positive role models from the past.

Write a lullaby for the new baby. We did this for each of our children, incorporating into four simple lines each child's name and some thoughts about what their coming meant to us. You can create a new melody or borrow the tune of an old folksong or hymn.

Create a birthday time capsule for each of your children. On the day a child is born, purchase a heavy molded plastic file box and fill it with books and periodicals that will provide a "snapshot" of the world as it was that day. Include

• the local newspaper from the child's hometown for the day of birth.

• a national newspaper for the same day.

• a current magazine focusing on prominent people.

• a current science magazine.

• several current special interest magazines, such as periodicals focusing on religion, sports, fashions, or politics.

• a world almanac for the year.

Years from now, the children who own these capsules will be fascinated to get a glimpse of the world as it was when they arrived on the scene. And the children whose birth was celebrated with this and other family traditions will have tangible evidence that theirs was a welcome arrival.

24 ■ Show Your Appreciation on Birthdays

Birthdays are splashy events in our home, even for those of us old enough to wish we had fewer candles on our cake. Traditions accompanying this family milestone are especially helpful for building self-esteem because they offer us a chance to affirm the growth and uniqueness of each family member. When we take time to recognize someone's birthday, we're saying to that person, "There's no one else quite like you—you're God's special gift to the world."

In Addition to Cake   Candle-topped cakes, ice cream, parties, and presents are standard fare for most birthdays in American homes. Add one or more of the following traditions:

Gather around the birthday person's bed in the morning.   Wake him or her by singing "Happy Birthday" and presenting flowers, cards, and gifts.

Decorate the person's place at the family dining table.   Use balloons, crepe paper, and a special plate or placemat.

Bake surprises inside the birthday cake. Wrapped in wax paper, these treats can be coins, jewelry, a little toy, or something more mischievous.

Have a traditional birthday tablecloth. Give party guests colored, indelible pens so they can autograph the tablecloth, adding the date as well. Use the cloth again each year for the person's birthday celebration, adding new names and repeating the old ones.

Have birthday interviews each year with your children. Using a video or audiocassette recorder, ask questions that will get them talking about their world: friends, hobbies, teachers, goals—even favorite foods, toys, and TV programs.

Bring out old photos and home videos of the birthday boy or girl. Baby pictures are especially fun to look at together and will spark some good memories.

Give each child a new privilege and responsibility on each birthday reflecting another year of maturity. The new "status" can be as simple as a later bedtime hour for a smaller child or as significant as a driver's license for a sixteen-year-old.

Write a birthday letter each year to the person being honored. Praise his or her qualities and accomplishments that make you proud. Talk about the challenges the person may face in the coming year and express your support in meeting them. Close with a prayer. Find a quiet moment alone to read the letter together, then save it in a special file.

25 ■ Mark Your Child's Coming of Age

In many cultures of the world, traditions provide for a "coming of age" ceremony that marks an official passing from childhood to adulthood. The Jewish community, for example, observes the bar mitzvah for young men and the bas mitzvah for young women. The rituals allow older family members and friends to say, "We welcome you to take your place among us as an adult."

Recognizing Adulthood In the absence of such a community rite, young people often are left wondering when they can expect to be recognized as an adult. For that reason, even though our two children have yet to reach their teenage years, we're already planning to officially and publicly welcome each of them as an adult. Here are the plans we're making now:

A key talk Our children have received ongoing sex education since they were quite young. But when the day comes—probably in their early teen years—that we feel they're ready, we intend to have what some of our friends have dubbed a "key talk."

To observe this tradition, the child and the parent of the same gender find an intimate setting to have an in-depth conversation summing up the parents' perspective on God's gift of sexuality and the need to remain sexually pure. The child is also encouraged to ask any lingering questions about sexuality and romance.

The talk culminates with the child's making an explicit covenant with God to remain a virgin until marriage. To seal the covenant, the parent gives the child a ring to wear symbolizing the "key" to his or her heart and reminding the child of his or her commitment. (For more information on the key talk, see the book *Raising Them Chaste* by Richard and Renée Durfield, Bethany House, 1991.)

A coming of age party   More public will be the coming of age party we plan to throw for each of our children. Like a bar or bas mitzvah, this celebration will invite extended family members and friends to join us in recognizing the young person's adulthood with gifts and a ceremony. It includes:

- brief speeches by some of those who attend, affirming the young person's character, maturity, and potential for a happy and fruitful life.

- a charge from us as parents to continue walking with God for a lifetime.

- a time of prayer and spoken blessings, with the laying on of hands by the adults in attendance.

- a gift from us that will serve as a lifelong reminder of the day.

A letter   In preparation for their coming of age celebrations, we want to write letters to our children expressing our joy in watching them mature over the years, our pleasure in welcoming them to adulthood, and our hopes for their enjoying a long, happy, and prosperous life. In the letters we'll note the character qualities, talents, skills, and experiences our children possess that make us confident of their continuing success.

A scrapbook   In the meantime, we've started a file of our favorite sayings, quotations, Bible verses, advice on various subjects, anecdotes, and even cartoons that best express the values, priorities, and principles we believe are critical for a godly approach to life. When our children come of age, we'll present the material to them organized into a scrapbook as a source of counsel, insight, and encouragement. We expect this particular gift to become a treasured possession.

With coming of age traditions like these, we hope to help our children move confidently into adulthood.

26 ■ Reaffirm Your Love on Wedding Anniversaries

Paul's parents knew how to have fun kicking up their heels in a ballroom. So they observed a simple but beautiful tradition: they went dancing on every wedding anniversary. Every year, no matter what else they did, they were always sure to get out on a dance floor to enjoy at least one song together.

One year when he was a child, however, their finances were just too tight for an evening out. Rather than abandon what had become for them a treasured custom, his parents went outside, turned the car radio on, and danced together in the moonlight. Many years later, Paul still remembers vividly how they waltzed around the backyard that night—a testimony to the significance that particular family tradition had for him as well as for them.

Making Anniversaries Special Most couples observe at least a few wedding anniversary customs: perhaps a bouquet of flowers for the wife, dinner out, a gift or two. Add to these a few traditions tailor-made for your marriage, and you'll find the day becomes more meaningful—and more romantic—than ever.

Romantic music   Music can play a big part in celebrating an anniversary. If you've always called one particular tune "your song," arrange ahead of time for it to be played at the restaurant where you eat out. If your celebration is at home, get a record or tape of that song and others that were popular while you were dating, and play them while you remember old times together.

Wedding memories   If you made an audiotape, home movie, or videotape of your wedding ceremony, relive the excitement of the day by playing it again every anniversary. Break out the wedding album, photos, and guest book.

Retell the story of your romance, engagement, and wedding to your children. Encourage them to ask questions, and emphasize how much in love you grew to be—and still are. Talk about the beauties and benefits of marriage.

Don't forget both the romantic and the funny moments of your story—kids seem to like these best. When we tell our children about our wedding, we describe in detail the romantic beach setting of the ceremony. And we laugh together about how a relative took so long to decorate the getaway car, most of the guests were gone before he came back with it—and we were left sitting, all forlorn, on the street curb. (He hasn't decorated any cars since.)

27 ■ Commemorate Past Milestones with Anniversary Celebrations

Weddings aren't the only milestones worthy of an anniversary celebration. Think back over your years as a family to the happy events that stand out in your memory.

Other Anniversaries Consider these possibilities for unusual anniversary celebrations:

Spiritual birthdays Can you or other family members trace the beginning of your life as a committed Christian to a particular date? If so, celebrating that spiritual birthday with your family can reaffirm your faith, allow opportunity to reflect on your personal growth, and give you a chance to discuss what it means to be a Christian.

While some family members may be able to point to a particular date of "rebirth," others may not because they were raised from the beginning to know the Lord. If that's the case in your home, don't let these family members feel cheated. Celebrate the day they were baptized or dedicated to God as children.

The day you and your spouse met   Do you remember the date and the details of the occasion? If so, you can memorialize the event with an anniversary observance of some sort—perhaps with an annual visit to the place where it happened.

Your first date   If you can remember the details of your first date, try celebrating its anniversary by recreating it. If you went to the beach, do it again. If you saw a movie, see if you can rent the video for the evening. If you went to a restaurant, eat there again or order the same meal somewhere else. If you can recall bits and pieces of your conversation that night, go over what you said and talk about the impressions you made on each other.

The day you moved into your present home   Is your present home a beloved spot where you've shared lots of memories? Then celebrate the anniversary of the day you moved in. Get out old photos with your home in the background and take some time as a family to remember how it looked when you first came, as well as the various transformations it has survived since that time.

You may think of other past events that you want to keep alive in your family's memory. Whatever milestones are meaningful to you are fair game for a celebration—and a new tradition.

28 ■ Put Down Roots in Your New Home

We lived in ten different homes in three different states during the first two years of our marriage. Since then we've made seven more moves, two of them across the continent.

It may sound as if we make a tradition of moving itself, but the truth is that we've come to see how family traditions as a whole can ease the stress of relocation by providing a degree of continuity and stability at home—wherever that home may be.

Make Moving Easier A few particular family customs, adopted as a kind of ritual for moving, can keep stress from becoming distress.

Solidify friendships in the place you're leaving. Give your family a chance to grieve the separation honestly and openly.

Invite your closest friends to a party or a dinner held for the explicit purpose of saying goodbye. Spend the evening remembering old times and planning ways to stay in touch across the miles.

Buy your younger children autograph books and your older children address books. Then encourage them to have their friends sign them or record their addresses in them.

Take the family ahead of time on an inspection trip to your new home. While there you can do some things to help you start feeling at home:

- Join hands to pray a blessing on the dwelling.

- Spend some relaxed time in the house—perhaps hanging a few pictures and setting out a few familiar objects that can provide a sense of continuity.

- Explore the surrounding area.

- Meet new people in the neighborhood.

Reestablish as quickly as possible your family's normal routine. Observe the traditions you're accustomed to. Don't neglect the nightly blessing, the weekly family night, or the table grace song.

Hold a new home dedication ceremony, inviting friends, neighbors, and church acquaintances in your new area. It need not be complicated. Just choose a few appropriate verses of Scripture, such as Psalms 121:8 and 127:1; prepare a prayer of dedication; and have some light snacks on hand.

Through it all, keep an adventurous spirit! God has new horizons, new relationships, and new experiences in store for your family in your new home.

29 ■ Celebrate a Bright Future for Newlyweds

After birth and death, the most important milestone in most people's lives is their wedding day. Our children won't be old enough to marry until several years from now, but when the big day comes, we want to be ready to help them celebrate in a way they'll never forget.

Wedding Traditions Most of the wedding plans, of course, will be made by the couple themselves. But in addition to whatever customs they may choose to observe, we hope to contribute a few traditions of our own, borrowed from our own wedding day and from the celebrations of our friends. Here are some of the more memorable customs we have in mind:

A special wedding shower Friends gave us a joint bride and groom shower. Ahead of time, our pastor secretly borrowed childhood pictures and home movies from our parents. Then he put together a humorous and wildly fictional story of our lives up to that point, illustrating it with pictures that were guaranteed to make us both blush. The final product was projected on a screen at the shower using a home movie projector and an opaque projector. This pre-wedding event was so much fun we can't wait to make it a tradition in our family.

Gifts for new in-laws Leisa has developed two practical shower gifts perfect for future in-laws. She collects the groom's favorite recipes to give to the bride, or vice-versa if the groom will be doing most of the cooking. She gathers them from parents, siblings, and friends who are most likely to know the person's tastes. Then she writes them on printed recipe cards and places them in a small file box. Warning: This gift should come from someone other than the future mother-in-law—it might be interpreted as a criticism of someone's cooking!

Leisa also likes to buy a calendar and mark on it all the birthdays, anniversaries, and other special dates of the bride's or groom's extended family. Then we present it to that person's spouse-to-be. That way, the new couple will be sure to impress everyone with their ability to remember all those special family days.

The wedding ceremony Instead of having the bride's father give her away, we took our cue from an old Jewish custom and had both sets of parents accompany the bride and groom down the aisle. (Actually, they walked across the sand dunes—we got married on the beach.) We hope our children will consider doing the same, because it reflects more accurately what takes place in the hearts of all the parents involved as they release their children to build a new family.

A prayer of blessing One of the most memorable moments in our wedding was when all the members of both families gathered around us to pray a blessing on us. If a brief prayer time like this won't fit into the order of service for our children's weddings, perhaps they can let us carry on the tradition at the reception.

Some healthy laughter No wedding is complete without the customary pranks on the bride and groom. We keep them clean, harmless, and in good taste. When Paul was a groomsman for one of his graduate school buddies, he prepared an 8″ × 11″ version of the old Olympic score cards, with large black numbers like "9.5," "7.0," and so on. Each groomsman hid one of the cards inside his tux jacket, and when the groom kissed the bride at the end of the ceremony, the men held them up to "score" the kiss.

Years later, our friends are still laughing about that score. It's the kind of memory-making tradition we hope will fill both our children's wedding days.

30 ■ Adopt a Tradition from Your Ancestors' Homeland

In recent years, digging for family roots has become a popular pastime in America. Many of us want to learn about the ancestors who have to one degree or another helped to shape our identity—our values, our customs, our economic condition, our geographical location, even our physical endowments. Those who search out their family's history find that such labors reward them with a deeper sense of identity, connectedness, and appreciation for their heritage.

After tracing their family trees back to a particular part of the world, many people want to broaden their research to learn about the culture that shaped their ancestors. This kind of information may be especially important to a family who knows the general location of their ancestral home but is unable to reconstruct their specific lineage because the records necessary to do the research simply don't exist.

Ethnic Traditions   One way to celebrate your ethnic inheritance is to adopt a tradition from your ancestors' homeland. Consider these examples:

- Many families with Ukrainian roots have rediscovered their ancestors' folk art of dyeing Easter eggs in complex, brilliant-colored patterns.

- Chinese-Americans in many cities enjoy celebrating the Chinese New Year with fireworks and parades.

- African-American homes sometimes pass on storytelling traditions with ancestral tales such as "Why Mosquitoes Buzz in People's Ears" and legends of Anansi the spider.

- Families with Irish ancestors often observe St. Patrick's Day with church services, parades, the "wearin' of the green," and traditional Irish menus.

- Children with a Dutch or Belgian heritage may enjoy setting out shoes filled with hay on December 5th, the eve of St. Nicholas Day. Then their parents can continue the old custom of trading the hay for treats, claiming the next morning with a wink that the good saint brought the gifts and his horse ate the hay.

For more ideas, visit the public library.

31 ∎ Publish an Extended Family Newsletter

A few years ago, our extended family stretched across three continents—North America, Europe, and Asia. Although we're a bit closer together now, we're still scattered from Florida to Maryland and from Georgia to Arkansas. Counting only our first cousins, we represent at least ten states.

Nor is our situation unusual. Living in central Florida, where more than 80 percent of the population was born in another state, we're keenly aware that our generation has given the term *extended family* a whole new meaning.

Staying in Touch How do you stay in touch across the miles? The phone is a marvelous invention, but the costs of long-distance calls add up quickly. For that reason, many extended families have established the tradition of a newsletter to stay involved in one another's lives and to maintain a sense of their common heritage.

The effort can be as simple or as comprehensive as you want to make it. Here's a strategy.

Survey your relatives by phone or by mail to see who is interested in taking part. Tell them you want to begin circulating among them a packet of family news to be updated every time it goes around. Remember to include shut-ins, those living alone, and relatives you haven't heard from in a while.

Request address corrections and name changes. If you survey by mail, enclose a stamped, self-addressed envelope with each inquiry.

Ask for suggestions in shaping the venture, and set a deadline for relatives to respond. But don't pressure anyone to join—those who reluctantly agree to take part, perhaps because they lack interest or feel too busy, will be likely to break the chain or delay the letter, causing frustration for everyone else.

Near the deadline date, plot the best mail route for those who wish to be included. If you receive survey letters after the deadline, simply plot a new route the second time around.

Arrange the names and addresses on your list according to your projected route, with your own name first and last so everything will come back to you. Then write a letter welcoming all the participants to the new family publishing enterprise.

Enclose with the letter items such as

- a brief update of news from your branch of the family.
- current snapshots.

- any item that refers to a recent activity or accomplishment of someone in your home.

- a favorite recipe.

- clippings or photocopies of an excerpt from an interesting article or book you've read.

- a good quote, joke, or riddle you'd like to pass on.

Don't forget to enclose a copy of the mail route. Include instructions on how long each family is allowed to keep the packet before sending it to the next home. Remind them that the packet will increase in weight for a while and then level off as family members replace their old material with new.

Make a file marked "Family Newsletter." Whenever you come across an item you'd like to include the next time around, you'll have a place to store it until the packet comes back—full of fascinating tidbits about the lives of loved ones who no longer feel so far away.

32 ■ Build a Repertoire of Traditional Songs

One of the richest elements of any culture is its heritage of music. Sadly enough, young people have the lazy habit of idolizing whatever batch of songs happens to blast from the radio just now. Recent styles of popular music—rock, rap, heavy metal—are crowding out the music of earlier generations as if the older songs were somehow obsolete.

Worse yet, the parents of many of these young people had the same attitude when they were teenagers. The result is that in some homes, there's little appreciation for any music produced before the 1950s.

How do we overcome this kind of cultural narrowness? Our family has chosen to avoid the repetitious fare of popular radio stations and to listen instead to music from a variety of styles and periods. To be sure, we have our favorite types of music, and those favorites differ among us. But as we broaden our tastes, all of us are learning how much our culture's musical heritage has to offer.

Sing Together   Our approach to reconnecting
with the music of earlier generations includes the
development of a repertoire of traditional songs we
sing as a family. We learn these songs and sing
them together

- in church worship services.

- while riding in the car, especially on long
  trips.

- at family mealtimes and children's bedtime.

- while doing chores, which seem to go faster
  when we sing.

- at play, especially when we take part in traditional children's games that require singing.

- during holiday seasons with their own music.

To cultivate your family's musical heritage, you
can make a tradition of family singing. Here is a
list of the kinds of songs to consider, along with a
few examples of our favorite tunes:

Hymns   "Holy, Holy, Holy"; "O For a Thousand
Tongues"; "A Mighty Fortress Is Our God"; "Jesus
Loves Me"; "Fairest Lord Jesus"; "Amazing
Grace."

Patriotic songs   "The Star-Spangled Banner";
"America the Beautiful"; "My Country 'Tis of
Thee."

Bedtime songs   Brahms' "Cradle Song"; "Rock-a-Bye Baby"; "Hush Little Baby, Don't You Cry."

Rounds and story songs   "Row, Row, Row Your Boat"; "Three Blind Mice"; "Are You Sleeping, Brother John?"; "Dona Nobis Pacem"; "High Hopes."

Regional songs and folk songs   "Old John Henry"; "Clementine"; "The Yellow Rose of Texas"; "Goober Peas"; "When Johnny Comes Marching Home Again"; "The Erie Canal"; "Old Folks at Home."

Play and nonsense songs   "The Farmer in the Dell"; "London Bridge"; "Oh, Where, Oh, Where Has My Little Dog Gone?"; "The Muffin Man"; "Shoo, Fly, Don't Bother Me"; "Take Me Out to the Ballgame"; "In the Good Old Summertime"; "The Bear Went Over the Mountain."

For more songs to sing as a family, look for books and recordings at your public library.

If one of you can accompany the rest of the family on a musical instrument, that's all the better. But we've found that a capella voices sound fine. Either way, a tradition of family singing will open the door to appreciating the time-tested music that's richer than you may have imagined.

33 ■ Display Family Portraits and Heirlooms

Most homes have accumulated at least a few objects that tell their family history: old photos, books, keepsakes, or even household items passed down so many generations that they are now antiques. These memorabilia left to us by our ancestors form a kind of tangible tradition that links us to them. Stubborn survivors of the ravages of time, they represent to us the everyday realities of years gone by more concretely than written accounts or even pictures can.

Invested with personal and historical meaning, such inherited items deserve a place of honor in our homes. Yet many portraits and keepsakes lie forgotten in dusty corners of the attic or under a bed—rusting, mildewing, crumbling, or otherwise fading from our family history. They await our rediscovery, and they promise a rich reward of enhanced family identity if we make the effort to preserve them and put them on display.

Family History Treasures Survey the items from the past in your home. You might be surprised at how much you find. Here's a list of just a few of the articles turned up by our family:

- Old portraits from several generations back
- An antique, hand-cranked sausage mill used in a meat market owned by Paul's family when he was a child
- Old meat-cutting tools used by Paul's father
- An antique fire extinguisher
- Antique glass dishes passed on by Leisa's grandmother
- Heirloom quilts handmade by Leisa's great-grandmother
- An antique trunk

We also found several household items, passed on by various relatives that now qualify as antiques: a nut grinder, a copper pot, a wicker laundry basket, a cookie jar, a cream pitcher, an old typewriter, Depression glass, postcards, and coins.

Once you've made your own list, think about how each item could be displayed somehow in your home. Consider the following possibilities:

Shelves and display cabinets Our china cabinet features our antique glass pieces. Along the top of our kitchen wall is a built-in shelf where we show off items like Leisa's antique trunk—out of which is trailing a trio of old quilts.

Tables and desk tops   In our house, an old copper pot holds stray pennies on an office desk. The antique typewriter graces the top of a set of drawers in the same room.

Walls   Photos might be grouped with other items, such as framed and matted antique postcards or coins. Small kitchen utensils and workshop tools make interesting three-dimensional wall decorations. We've seen heirloom quilts hung on the wall as well.

You can also show off family treasures by giving them new uses. Our antique fire extinguisher and the old sausage mill now hold potted plants. Old utility pole transistors provide us with paper weights. A hundred-year-old laundry basket provides one of our daughter's dolls with a bed.

Once you've surveyed your ancestral artifacts, catalog them in a hardbound theme book or card file. Make notations about their age, their origin, their function, and any family anecdotes associated with them. When you pass them on to the next generation, your children will be grateful that this information wasn't lost. In time, your catalog may even become a piece of history itself.

34 ■ Hold a Family Reunion

The farther extended families scatter, the more important the tradition of family reunions becomes. No other event is so capable of giving families a feeling of connectedness and uniqueness.

Reunion Activities You can find several helpful books on how to plan family reunions at the public library. You can even hire professional reunion planners for the job if you desire. Because those excellent resources are available, we won't attempt to offer a comprehensive guide for putting one together. But we will mention a few basic activities you might want to include in a large family get-together:

A family history book Several months before the event, invite relatives to submit brief histories of their families, including favorite family anecdotes. Collect them into a single book, and sell copies at the reunion for a small price to cover the expenses of making it.

Oral history sessions   Have older family members speak about their past while a cassette recorder is running. Send them a list of questions such as these ahead of time so they can be prepared:

- What do you remember about your parents, grandparents and great-grandparents?

- What was daily life like when you were a child?

- What were the most memorable events of your childhood?

- What word of advice would you give to younger generations?

A family recipe book   Ask each family to contribute several favorite recipes. Collect them ahead of time, then sell a photocopied cookbook with a title like "Thigpen Family Favorites."

A family art and talent show   Display artwork by family members, and feature your family's singers, musicians, dancers, actors, and comedians on stage.

A family quilt   Have each nuclear family use fabric paint to decorate a precut quilt square and write their names on it. Then sew the squares together to create a family quilt that you can pass each year from home to home.

The honoring chair Have an honoring chair session (see chapter 48) for the eldest family member present or the recognized matriarch or patriarch of the clan.

A worship service Set aside time to sing old hymns, thank God for your family and your heritage, and focus on spiritual values.

Historical readings Listen to family members reading from journals, diaries, correspondence, or other written works from your ancestors that touch on your heritage as a family.

A group photograph Family reunions usually provide the only opportunities to get a picture of the extended family. Take a group photo at each reunion so that you can watch how your family changes over the years. Announce the time early so that everyone can make plans to be included.

A master mailing list A reunion is the perfect time to compile an up-to-date extended family mailing list. Use it to notify folks about other events or to start a family newsletter (see chapter 31).

Plan the next reunion At the end of the event, take a survey to find out when folks would like to gather again. Solicit volunteers on the spot—while they're still excited about what they've just experienced—to plan the next reunion. By the time everyone sets out for home, you'll have a wealth of new memories to share and a new appreciation for your extended family ties.

35 ■ Make a Pilgrimage to Family Historical Sites

The best novelists know that they have to provide in their works a sense of "place." Vivid, concrete details in the setting of a novel allow readers to conncct cmotionally with the story—to see, hear, touch, taste, and smell what is described.

That same sense of "place" plays a role in our attempts to connect with history. Most Christians who have toured the Holy Land, for example, would probably agree that the Bible came alive in new ways for them after they made the visit. A firsthand experience of the terrain, the climate, the architecture, and the atmosphere of a place makes it easier to imagine the events that took place there, however distant in the past.

A Family History Pilgrimage The Christian community has long recognized this reality through the tradition of pilgrimages. A pilgrimage is a journey to a place that has been set apart by its connection with some noteworthy person or event. A *spiritual* pilgrimage usually takes us to a holy place associated with a miracle or a saint. A *family history* pilgrimage, on the other hand, takes us to a place connected with some significant part of our family's past.

We want the stories of our predecessors to be real to our children. When we told them, for example, that their ancestor Jone Phippen sailed into Jamestown almost four centuries ago on a cramped wooden boat, we wanted them to be able to smell the brine and hear the waves lapping against the hull. So we took them to Virginia to visit the reconstruction of that early settlement, complete with replicas of the passenger ships.

Most parents probably take their own family history pilgrimages without calling them that. When they drive by their old high school with their kids in the car, they may point out the classroom where the chemistry experiment went haywire. When they visit Grandma's house out in the country, they may show the kids the swimming hole where they spent many lazy summer days.

What some families do spontaneously can become even more meaningful if it's cultivated intentionally as a family tradition. With a little planning, you can root your children more firmly in their heritage by taking them on pilgrimages to places like these:

Historical sites connected to your family   Did your ancestors come into the country at Ellis Island? Did a relative fight in the Battle of Gettysburg? Did someone in your family take part in the California Gold Rush? Take your children to the places where these things happened.

Geographical sites somehow involved in your family history   One of Paul's ancestors was lost in the Great Dismal Swamp of North Carolina and never heard from again. We want to take our children there and tell how it happened.

Cemeteries where ancestors are buried   Your family can learn more than birth and death dates from the inscriptions on their gravestones.

Places frequented by you, your parents, and your grandparents   Take the kids to see the old family farm; the houses where you and other relatives lived, the schools and churches you attended, the businesses you patronized, the parks where you played; and the places where you used to "hang out" as a teenager.

Places made significant by a particular event   Show your children the home or hospital where you or other relatives were born, the restaurant where you and your spouse had your first date, the spot where you became engaged, and the chapel where you were married.

Make a family history pilgrimage at least once a year. It's a tradition that's guaranteed to make your children's heritage come alive.

36 ■ Create Family Archives

Governments, corporations, and other organizations that want to maintain a record of their history typically create a set of archives. These collections of important documents may include anything from maps to financial records to photographs.

Families who want to leave a lasting record of their life together can create their own archives. Organize a designated file drawer, cabinet, or shelf space to hold the relevant materials according to the categories most meaningful to you. Preserve documents in file folders, boxes, scrapbooks, manila envelopes, albums, or periodical containers.

We suggest two broad divisions of your material: records from earlier generations and records of your ongoing family life. The first category includes items from your parents and their ancestors: photos, diaries, correspondence, legal and financial records—anything of interest to you in creating a record of their lives. The second group should contain the kinds of memorabilia families often keep in scrapbooks: birth announcements, obituaries, children's artwork and essays, school report cards, and so on.

You can further categorize in two ways: either

according to the type of document or according to the subject matter. Types of documents might include these:

- Photos

- Standard-sized (usually $8^1/_2'' \times 11''$) printed, typed, or handwritten materials

- Irregular-sized printed or handwritten materials

- Newspaper and magazine clippings

- Journals and diaries

- Audiocassettes, videocassettes, and home movies

If you prefer, group materials by subject matter. Be aware that this approach requires more space. Here are some suggested categories:

People   Create one file for each person. In this system, for example, you place your grandfather's journal, portrait, and correspondence in a single box or file while your child's report cards, artwork, and birthday party invitation fill another.

Correspondence   Arrange letters either chronologically or by recipient.

Legal records   File birth certificates, death certificates, marriage licenses, and business documents together.

Artistic creations and performances Include drawings, original poetry, and videotapes of plays or concerts in this group.

Birthdays, anniversaries, and holidays Create a file or box devoted to memorabilia from celebrations of each occasion.

Make sure materials are stored out of direct sunlight and in a place not subject to temperature extremes, water leaks, or infiltration by pests. Handle them with clean hands and keep them away from food and drink.

Establishing archives might sound like a big project, but you don't have to do it all at once. Make one file or box at a time. As new materials appear, put them in a large box and then sort a few whenever you have a spare moment.

Someday your descendants will thank you for your efforts. Because a tradition is something handed down, creating family archives is one tradition that will preserve many others—allowing a record of your family's values and uniqueness to be passed on to the next generation.

37 ■ Double the Honor of an Accomplishment

Back in the days when public schools still routinely administered corporal punishment, many households had a firm rule: "If you get in trouble at school, you'll have more trouble waiting for you when you get home." That way, the spankings—and the motivation to behave correctly—were always doubled.

We won't attempt to debate the wisdom of that approach to discipline. But we can say that a similar policy with regard to honoring the *praiseworthy* behavior of family members doubles their motivation to work hard toward their goals.

Additional Honors Whenever possible, attend the program or ceremony at which a family member receives an award. Then add your own celebration in recognition of the accomplishment. Consider these tips for doubling the honor a family member receives:

Photograph or videotape the award ceremony. If you take an especially memorable shot, have it enlarged and framed as a gift for the honoree.

After the event, hold your own family celebration and invite friends. Throw a small party to recognize a job promotion, the sterling performance on stage, the announcement of a scholarship, or the election to an office in student government.

Put your family member in the news when he or she does something noteworthy. Talk to the feature editor of your community newspaper or to the editor in charge of the specific news area involved—sports, religion, business. If the newspaper won't carry the story as a feature, put it in the paper as a personal ad in the classified section. Simply include a photo of the honoree, a one-sentence statement of congratulations, and a signature of family names.

Put your congratulations in writing. Compose a letter to the person honored that expresses your pride in his or her achievements and your confidence that success will continue. Note especially the character qualities in the person that contributed to the accomplishment, such as perseverance, self-discipline, or patience.

Designate a permanent place to display awards. Choose a corner of a room where you can hang photos, framed certificates, and plaques on the wall and show off trophies and ribbons on a shelf.

"Rejoice with those who rejoice" (Rom. 12:15) is a biblical instruction our family has turned into a tradition.

38 ■ Hold a Family Award Ceremony

Sometimes the world doesn't recognize achievements that deserve praise. Who gives out trophies for a well-tended vegetable garden? a big improvement in math skills in just a semester? surviving sleepless nights with a colicky baby?

Everyone in your home is an unsung hero of one kind or another. So honor family members with an annual family award ceremony. This tradition can be serious or lighthearted, recognizing anything from a child's joyful mastery of the bicycle to a parent's agonizing but successful weight-loss efforts.

Recognize Family Accomplishments

Let each person keep a private notebook of family accomplishments observed, jotting down a possible award whenever some quiet success comes to his or her attention. Focus on the victories of achievement and endurance that won't be recognized by anyone else. Look for accomplishments such as these:

Personal goals   Recognize personal goals fulfilled, such as reading a certain number of books in a single summer, reaching a particular yearly grade average, or beating the sales record for the previous year.

Actions that demonstrate character   Give service awards for maintaining an elderly neighbor's yard, consistently showing patience to younger siblings, or helping parents with chores above and beyond the call of duty.

Admirable efforts that didn't gain top billing   A person's family may be the only ones who know just how much hard work, sacrifice, and commitment went into the science fair project that didn't grab a ribbon, the exam preparation that didn't earn a top grade, or the football game that didn't end in victory. Present an award for what really counts: the diligent effort to give it all.

Whimsical honors   Include a few humorous awards that show your appreciation for the labors of daily family life: Fastest Toy-Picker-Upper, Most Dishes Washed at a Single Meal, or Most Trips Made to the Supermarket on a Single Day.

If you like, invite relatives or close friends to join you for the ceremony along with a "banquet" in your home. Dress your best for the occasion and ham it up when you make your presentations. The evening will be so full of fun and appreciation that you'll be eager to make it an annual event.

39 ■ Display Your Family's Masterpieces

Walk through our home just now, and you'll find almost every room functioning as part of our family art gallery. In the family room you can see our son's modeling clay sculptures displayed on their own special table. On the kitchen counter sits our daughter's handmade basket. The refrigerator door is covered with the children's crayon drawings. A poster of the cover on Paul's recent novel towers over a bookcase. Several rooms sparkle with the bright floral prints of Leisa's fabric creations—window treatments, cushions, and bedcovers.

Your family no doubt enjoys the same creative urges ours does. So what are you doing with the resulting masterpieces? Are they admired for a moment and then tucked away in a drawer or up in the attic? Or do you put them on display so that your family and others can enjoy them for a while?

Family Art Gallery   If you want to show off your family creativity, try these ideas for making your home a gallery:

Walls and doors are the most obvious places to display two-dimensional art. Designate a single wall, door or window as your gallery. If it's in a child's room, consider filling the area entirely with artwork as a sort of homemade wallpaper. Or purchase a nice picture frame with glass and perhaps a neutral mat, sized to fit an $8^1/2'' \times 11''$ picture. Encourage your children to draw on paper that size and display a different creation every week in the same frame.

Glass-topped tables provide another display area for drawings and paintings. Just slip them under the glass. These tables can also accommodate sculptures and free-standing crafts.

Put functional items to use, even when they don't quite fit the rest of your home's decor. However crude they may seem to some people, those handmade pencil cans, bookmarks, jewelry boxes, hot pads, and Christmas tree ornaments have a charm all their own.

When your child designs an especially impressive structure with building blocks or other construction toys, set it out for display in a prominent place. When he or she wants to use the materials again, take a snapshot before the demolition takes place. Do the same with domino designs, modeling clay figures, or any other creation destined to be recycled. Then fill a photo album with your child's masterpieces.

When too many drawings and paintings accumulate, as they inevitably will, share them with people outside your family. Designate a drawer to keep the artwork for later use as greeting cards, stationery, or even gift wrap. Relatives, close friends, and your children's peers will enjoy the homemade touch.

Displaying your family members' arts and crafts says to them, "I enjoy the beautiful things you make. I cherish your creativity." So make it your custom to show off their masterpieces. Your obvious pride in what they do will build their self-esteem and encourage them to keep up the good work.

40 ■ Cultivate Unique Family Expressions

Every family develops its own jargon—a collection of words and phrases with private, shared meanings. Over the years, shared stories and poems, funny personal incidents, and childish renditions of difficult terms can enrich a home's vocabulary, creating new words, strange sayings, and unique twists of meaning. The resulting family idiom gives us a stronger sense of family identity and draws us closer together like a shared secret.

New Vocabulary In our home, for example, we use jargon like this:

- *Smackerels*—small bites of food, a term we picked up from reading *Winnie the Pooh*

- *Capooter*—our personal computer, because that's what came out in our daughter's first attempt to pronounce the word

- *Love sammich*—a family hug—with parents on the outside and kids squeezed between (*sammich* is *sandwich* in south Georgia)

- *Epizoodee*—1) any malady that can't be otherwise diagnosed, as in "I don't feel like eat-

ing cauliflower 'cause I've got the epizoodee"; or 2) those funny little indentations
on your skin left by clothes that are too tight

- *Ogriety*—grouchiness, from the root word *ogre*

- *Usgustable*—something particularly ugly, dis-
gusting, and reprehensible

- *Groach*—a contraction for *gross cockroach,* a
particularly *usgustable* sort we often encounter here in the South

- *Shaky cheese*—grated Parmesan shaken out
of a can, a term our son borrowed from the
boy across the street

As you can see, family jargon can have a variety
of sources. But wherever these words and phrases
come from, they take on special meaning through
repetition. In that way, they become a spoken custom, as much a part of our family tradition as a
holiday ritual.

To make the most of this verbal tradition, we
encourage families to pay attention to their jargon
and keep a record of it. The very act of seeking
out, recording, and talking over the words will help
firmly establish them as playful habits and multiply
the fun of your family's unique way of talking.

41 ■ Compile a Baby Talk Dictionary

Children never tire of hearing stories about themselves, especially tales of their antics when they were quite young. Those humorous anecdotes, woven into the fabric of the family legend, become a reminder of their own human uniqueness.

Kids' Jargon The funniest stories about little children usually revolve around something they once said. In fact, soon after our first child began talking, we realized that we'd be losing some wonderful memories if we didn't start recording the cute little expressions she coined. We jotted them down on slips of paper and tossed them in a file.

When our son came along, we added his babblings to the list of funny words and sayings "out of the mouths of babes"—items that in many cases went on to become part of our family jargon. To give you an idea of the result, here's a sampling from our file, along with a few gems from other families:

- *Daniel-lions*—dandelions, a term influenced by the biblical story of Daniel in the lions' den

- *Samson and Saliva*—Samson and Delilah

- *Willy lights*—lily whites—that is, pale legs, especially noticeable here in the Sunshine State

- *Sneakers bar* or *Snookums bar*—our favorite chocolate candy

- *Smashed potatoes*—mashed potatoes, emphasizing that they should be without lumps

- *Macanoonis*—macaroni, especially the curly kind

- *College cheese*—cottage cheese

- *Quiltment*—a quilted garment

- *Your-ami*—the big city in south Florida, because our son thought we were calling it *My Ami*

- *Candy juice*—fruit punch

- *L-bone*—elbow

- *O-beast*—obese

- *Drismal*—dreary, dismal, and drizzly

- *Mowlawner*—lawnmower

- *Soul popper*—soap opera

- *Flutterbys*—butterflies

- *Help-icopter*—the emergency helicopter

- *Sub-blurbs*—subtitles in a foreign-language film

- *Bathtised*—baptised

- *The Holy Snackrament*—the Holy Sacrament

We also include in the file clever sayings of the kids, like our daughter's comment when her kickball went into the flower bed: "If that happens again, Mom's begonias will be-gone-ias."

With these items and others, we're building a "Baby Talk Dictionary" to enjoy as a family and share with others. Someday, we'll be able to hand it down as a verbal heirloom to our son and daughter so they can read it to *their* kids—and expand it with new entries from the next generation.

42 ■ Read Aloud Together

Reading aloud together has been a tradition in our home since our first child was still in arms. The habit has paid off handsomely; our children love books, enjoy word play, and take pleasure in stretching their vocabularies.

Yet another benefit of reading together is the influence of literature on our family jargon. Poetry has planted especially fertile seed in our children's minds, whether it's nursery rhymes, song lyrics, verse by classic poets, or psalms from the Bible. Again and again, we've come to adopt as our own the pleasant rhythms and beautiful word pictures we've found in books of verse.

Expressions from Literature Check your public library for books of poetry to read aloud. Here are some brief examples of the expressions that have found their way into our family's everyday conversations:

- When Paul sweats while working on his waistline, he borrows the line from A. A. Milne: "A bear, however hard he tries, grows tubby without exercise."

- On foggy days, we chant the old nursery rhyme: "One misty, moisty morning, when cloudy was the weather. . . ."

- When we get back from a shopping trip, someone inevitably repeats the expression from Mother Goose: "Home again, home again, jiggity jog."

- If one of the children stalls when asked to do something, Leisa quotes the refrain made famous by Dr. Seuss: "Marvin K. Mooney, won't you please go *now!*"

- In December we find ourselves calling out the farewell of St. Nicholas as imagined by Walter de la Mare: "Happy Christmas to all, and to all a good night!"

- When we pray, Charles Wesley's lovely hymn lyric comes easily to our lips: "Jesus, Lover of my soul."

Make a tradition of reading aloud at home, and you'll find a gold mine of expressions to enrich your family jargon—and to fertilize your minds.

43 ■ Show Your Love When Someone's Away from Home

Right now, our family is singularly blessed by the amount of time we get to spend together at home. Only rarely does either parent have to travel without the rest of the family. In fact, we both work at home and teach our children at home, so we're all accustomed to having one another around much of the time.

That makes for a close-knit family, and we're grateful. But it also means that on the few occasions when one of us has to be away from home, the rest of us miss that family member sharply.

Over the years we've gleaned a number of traditions from families who have learned how to cope with frequent separations. Though it's still true, as the old song says, that there's no place like home, we've found you can send a little "home" along with the traveler, and leave a little of the traveler at home. Here's how:

When You Take a Trip Before you leave on a trip, leave behind some tokens of your love.

Write small love notes or words of encouragement to each family member staying home. Tell them how much you'll miss them and assure them that they'll be in your thoughts and prayers. Then hide each note around the house where you know it will be found by the right person after you've left: under a pillow, in a medicine cabinet, in a lunchbox, tucked between the pages of a school textbook.

If you'll be gone for several days, buy a few inexpensive gifts, one for each family member, and gift wrap them. Leave them with instructions about when they should be opened—a different one each day. Small tokens such as bookmarks, stickers, hair bows, pens and pencils, crossword puzzle books, and small toys are little reminders of your appreciation for the rest of the family.

Tape a spoken message to your family on audiocassette. Break the talk into segments, one for each dinnertime you'll miss while you're gone. Tell some jokes or riddles; sing a silly song; talk about the business you'll be handling, the people you'll be seeing, and the places you'll be going on the trip. If you have small children, you might make a tape for bedtime rather than dinnertime. For each night you'll be away, read or tell a brief story, sing a song, and pray for each family member.

While you're on the trip, send each family member a postcard or an "I miss you" card.   Postcards of the place you're visiting will help the family picture your surroundings. If you won't have much time to write while you're on the road, prepare cards ahead of time with a brief message. Address and stamp them, and take them with you to mail while you're away. You might even mail them before you leave home so they'll arrive sooner.

Let Them Know They're Missed   If you're the one staying home, make sure a little bit of home goes with the traveler.

Write a few love notes and hide them in the traveler's luggage.   Put them where he or she is sure to find them. Note on the envelopes a time for each one to be opened—first thing in the morning, lunchtime, bedtime, or whenever.

Paint a large banner or sign that says, "Welcome Home—We Missed You!"   Use it to greet a family member coming back from a trip.

Of course, in addition to all these efforts you can run up a phone bill. But a few thoughtful family traditions for travelers will go a long way toward easing the pain of separation and building excitement for the time when you're all back together again.

44 ■ Take Your Child Out for a Regular Date

No matter how much time a family may spend together, parents and children still need frequent one-on-one fellowship. In that private setting, we have a better opportunity to open our minds, bare our hearts, and enjoy the kind of intimacy so necessary to emotional wholeness.

For that reason, we've made frequent dates alone with our kids a family tradition. We say "frequent," because it doesn't always work out to be a weekly or even a monthly event. But our children know we're committed to getting one-on-one with them, so they enjoy anticipating the times and help us remember when we're overdue for one.

Great Dates   Great dates can take you in a number of directions:

Movie and review   When one of us takes a child to see a movie, we try to stop off afterward for dessert and an evaluation of what we've seen. *Beauty and the Beast,* for example, sparked a lively discussion of how appearances can be deceiving.

Mealtime musings   Hold an in-depth conversation over a meal at a favorite restaurant, using one of the ideas in chapter 18 to get your child talking.

Zoo   Our son loves going to the zoo because of his abiding fascination with animals. Petting zoos are especially fun.

Rodeo, circus, or fair   Bring lots of pocket change —your child is sure to want a program, cotton candy, and a souvenir trinket of some kind.

Museum, planetarium, or art gallery   You don't want your date to feel like just another classroom lesson, but if your child especially enjoys history, science, or art, these are good choices.

Concert, play, or other performance   One of Paul's most memorable dates with our daughter took them to a local theater's production of *The Miracle Worker,* the story of Helen Keller's remarkable tutor, Annie Sullivan, which gave them ample material for discussion afterward. We also take advantage of the musical concerts offered at a local college.

Photographic expedition   Take two cameras and go out looking for interesting shots. Watch for animals and nice landscapes out in the country, fascinating faces or architecture in the city.

Beach walk   This is one of our daughter's favorite dates. We hunt for seashells, look for dolphins, and draw pictures or write love letters in the sand.

Nature hike In the woods, count how many different kinds of wildflowers, butterflies, trees, or birds you can spot.

Family-oriented entertainment center Check out one of those complexes that feature indoor playgrounds, rooms of plastic balls, video games, and snacks. These businesses usually encourage parents to join their kids in the fun.

Playground adventure Find a time of day when you're likely to have the playground to yourselves. Then instead of sitting back and watching, get on all the equipment along with your child and swing, climb, slide, and spin together.

Almost any activity works well for a date if it's something both parent and child enjoy. Be careful, however; you may be tempted to combine the occasion with school, business, or family responsibilities, but doing so usually steals the pleasure.

Wherever you go and whatever you do, keep in mind that the best date is a relaxed time with no agenda other than having fun and growing closer.

45 ■ Set a Place with a "You Are Special" Plate

Years ago we discovered a time-honored tradition observed by some families of early America: the red plate. Whenever someone deserved special praise or attention, whether a family member or guest, a red plate was set at that person's spot on the dinner table. The one-of-a-kind dish became a badge of honor that set apart the person's place for the evening.

In recent years a number of homes have adopted this custom, and several plates have been manufactured especially for the purpose. Some are simply solid red. Others come in various colors with the words "You Are Special Today" printed around the rim.

"You Are Special" Occasions These "You Are Special" dishes can pull frequent duty around the house:

- On birthdays
- On wedding anniversaries
- On Mother's Day and Father's Day

- To acknowledge a guest whose visit has been a blessing

- On ordinary days when some family member needs a word of encouragement

- To recognize a family member's outstanding achievement

One family we know even places this special plate on the Christmas dinner table in front of a seat that no one takes. There, it provides a reminder that the meal is served in honor of an unseen Guest—the Lord Jesus.

If you're unable to purchase an inscribed plate or even a solid red one, try making a placemat to be used for the same purpose. Use watercolors, crayons, or felt-tipped pens to write your own message of honor on paper or poster board cut to the appropriate size and shape. Then cover it on both sides with clear contact paper.

Whatever the occasion, the tradition of setting a "You Are Special" place can turn any meal into a banquet honoring someone you love.

46 ■ Encourage Someone Who's Sick

When a family member is sick, small kindnesses mean more than ever. Some folks prefer to be left alone in a quiet room to recuperate. Others would rather be camped out in the middle of the family's activity so that they don't miss anything.

"Sick Day" Traditions   Whatever the style of each person in your home, they're sure to appreciate one or more of these "sick day" traditions:

Serve an attractive meal tray in bed or on the couch. Use a bright napkin and fancy dishes. Give kids a crazy-shaped plastic straw. This would also be a good time to use a "You Are Special" plate (see chapter 45).

Prepare the food you normally serve in an unusual way.   Use cookie cutters to make toast with different shapes, or cut toast in triangles. Serve soup in a fancy mug instead of a bowl. For little children, provide a toothpick to spear small cubes of cheese, ham, chicken, or turkey.

Bring some cheer to the surroundings.   Pick wild-flowers or garden flowers for the bedside.

Help relieve boredom.   Find some interesting reading material, such as a favorite magazine from the supermarket rack. Or play a quiet thinking game or board game with the one who's sick. Older children and parents might enjoy crossword puzzles or trivia quizzes.

Gather the family around and pray for healing.   It's the most important thing you can do!

Create a bedside box for sick kids.   In a large cardboard box, collect items for arts and crafts projects: scissors, crayons, tape, string, glue, colored paper, old magazines, brass fasteners, bits of fabric, yarn, buttons, and old jewelry. As a first project, the child can decorate the box itself. To keep the box special, allow it to be used only on sick days.

Provide cassette tapes, record albums, or CDs of restful music.   If the sick person is on the couch near a VCR, rent a few low-key videos.

Give the sick person a bell or whistle to call for help from a secluded spot.   But make sure it's used only occasionally so you don't wear out everyone else.

"Sick day" traditions like these are well worth the few minutes of extra effort they require. They make the time fly, ease the discomfort, and reaffirm your family members' care for one another.

47 ■ Put Together a "Blue Light Special"

Sometimes we stumble upon a tradition simply by doing something we enjoy and deciding to repeat it. That's the case with what we call our "Blue Light Special." Years ago the family cooked up this idea for Leisa at the end of a particularly trying week. It was such a big hit that we've done it again and again—and not just for Leisa.

A Special Surprise Here's how the "Blue Light Special" works:

When someone in your house needs a break, call together the rest of the family to conspire with you. Keeping it a surprise is half the fun, so make sure any child you tell is old enough to keep a secret.

Sneak off to the supermarket with this shopping list in hand:

- Bubble bath
- Sparkling cider
- The person's favorite cheese and crackers

- Fresh fruit, such as strawberries or raspberries

- Confectioners' sugar (to dip the fruit in)

- Mixed nuts

- The person's favorite chips and dip

- A magazine he or she would enjoy

- A scented candle

- A single rose or small bouquet of other flowers

- A blue light bulb

After you've had one "Blue Light Special," you'll already have some of these items on hand, such as the light bulb, the candle, and the bubble bath.

Arrange to get the person out of the house for ten or fifteen minutes. If possible, get your surprise ready before he or she comes home from work. Otherwise, try our usual strategy: we ask a neighbor to call with some reason that the person has to come to their house for a few minutes.

Once the person is out of the house, act quickly. Set a small table next to the bathtub in the master bathroom. Then get out your best china, crystal, silver, and linen to set one place at the table. Arrange all the snacks on fancy serving dishes and place these on the table. Put the cider in a bucket of ice on the floor. Set the rose in a bud vase next to the food, with the magazine alongside. Place a cassette tape player in the room with a selection of relaxing music. Light the scented candle, and screw the blue light bulb into a small table lamp. Turn off the other lights or leave on a night-light if the room is too dark. Fill the tub with hot water and bubble bath. Leave a fluffy bath towel nearby.

When the person returns, let the whole family guide him or her to the bathroom and shout "Surprise!" Turn on the music, turn down the lights, and shut the door. Give the person all evening to relax alone while the rest of you go out or stay in another part of the house.

Give someone a "Blue Light Special" soon—and maybe the favor will be returned on a blue day when you need it most.

48 ■ Set Someone in the Honoring Chair

If an announcement were suddenly made around the globe that the world would end in an hour, every telephone line would be jammed with people calling loved ones to say all the things they'd never gotten around to saying before.

Why leave unsaid all the important things until it's too late? In our home, we want to make sure we have ample opportunity to tell one another how we feel. So we've established the tradition of the honoring chair.

Expressing Appreciation The concept is simple. We place a comfortable chair in the middle of the room, choose someone to sit in it, and then take turns telling that person why we're glad he or she is alive. When we're done, there's usually not a dry eye around.

To try it in your home, just follow these guidelines:

Give every person present at least one turn to honor the person in the chair through some brief comments. Don't force it; let people take turns as they're ready. If you have a period of silence between comments, relax. It's a good time for the meaning of the words to soak in before you go on.

Save criticism or complaints for later.   This is the time for positive statements that will build up and comfort the one listening. Focus on the good things:

- Character qualities and attitudes you appreciate and admire

- Personal accomplishments that have made you proud of that person

- Anecdotes from the person's life that illustrate the traits you describe

- The difference he or she has made in your own life

In short, say anything appreciative you've been reluctant to say before because you didn't want to embarrass the person.

When it's your turn to speak, stand or sit directly in front of the chair.   Face the person, make eye contact, and speak directly to him or her—not to the others in the room.

Don't hesitate to touch the person in an affirming way.   It's appropriate if it's comfortable for both of you. A squeeze of the hand, a hand on the shoulder, or a warm hug can reinforce your words.

Don't apologize for tears. Strong emotions are normal in this setting and should be accepted as an indication of how deeply the person in the chair is loved.

End by praying for the person. Thank God for him or her and mention specifically some of the admirable traits noted during the honoring session.

Honoring Occasions When should you use the honoring chair? Keep these occasions in mind:

Birthdays At a birthday party or dinner, talk especially about the past year of the honoree's life—the accomplishments, the goals met, and the character qualities you've observed.

Anniversaries Set your spouse in the chair and tell him or her all the reasons why you're glad to be married to such a remarkable person.

Farewell When you throw a going-away party for someone you love, have that person sit in the chair while all the guests tell what they'll miss the most about him or her.

Anytime Don't wait for a special occasion. Whenever you sense that someone in your family needs some affirmation and support, pull out the honoring chair and set the person down.

49 ■ Establish a Family Fund for Those in Need

Christians have long debated whether the Old Testament practice of tithing—giving 10 percent of our income back to God—provides a standard for today. We recognize that every family must follow their own conscience in the matter, keeping in mind God's generosity toward them. But from the beginning of our marriage, we agreed that we would tithe through the church. And because we see 10 percent as a *minimum* standard for giving back to the Lord, we chose long ago to set aside an additional percentage of our income to establish a small family benevolence fund.

The purpose of this ongoing fund is simple: we draw from it to bless those in need. Sometimes we've sent checks to relief organizations caring for famine victims in Africa. At other times we've sent money anonymously to a family whose breadwinner was unemployed. The benevolence fund has helped pay friends' doctor bills, supported Christian missionaries, contributed to ministry building funds, and even sent two youngsters to a theme park for a well-deserved day of fun. The only rules are that we can't spend the money on ourselves and we must try to keep the funds flowing rather than accumulating in the account.

Family Giving   No doubt most Christian families have their own strategies for giving, and some might think our approach is too rigid. We don't think our plan is the best for everyone, but it works well for us. Setting aside a fixed amount already designated for benevolence assures that we'll make a regular practice of giving, and we can always give more when it's needed.

We realize that we're sharing this family tradition with you at the risk of sounding boastful. But this particular custom has brought us so much joy and blessing, we're willing to take that risk so that you'll consider doing the same.

You may be thinking right away that this tradition would be unrealistic for most budgets. We suffer ups and downs in our finances just like everyone else, yet God is always faithful to take care of us (see Luke 6:38). Since we made this regular giving our policy from the beginning, we've never known what it's like to live on a budget that didn't include it, so we don't really miss the money we set aside. In fact, our daughter practices the same principle with her allowance, helping us every month to sponsor a child in South America. We hope it will help her grow up thinking it's normal to give that way.

50 ■ Make Houseguests Feel Like Royalty

We live halfway between Daytona Beach and Orlando, Florida—between the world's most famous beach and the nation's number-one tourist destination. So we've had people come to stay with us from as far away as Australia. We've even had folks, unacquainted with one another, come in from three different states on the same weekend!

Uncommon Courtesy When our guests come, we do our best to fulfill the biblical direction to practice hospitality (see Rom. 12:13) with sensitivity and even a little flair. In our home, we've developed a few traditions for making our guests feel as welcome and pampered as possible:

We paint or print on our computer a large banner that welcomes our guests by name. The banner, hung across the garage door, makes folks feel loved as soon as they turn into the driveway. If we aren't notified that guests are coming soon enough to make the large banner before they arrive, we create a small poster with the same message to hang on the front door. Sometimes we even create both.

Around the house we place small cards. The cards have printed sentiments like "We're glad you're here" or "Your friendship is special," and we put them in places where we know the guests will find them, such as on a stack of fresh linens, on their pillows, or on the bathroom mirror.

In the guest room, we make it a custom to set up these items:

- A toiletry basket with small samples in case the guests have forgotten or run out of something
- A fresh fruit basket with sweets and nuts as well
- A pitcher and water glasses in case they get thirsty during the night
- A homemade "Welcome to Florida" card
- A vase of fresh flowers
- A collection of brochures and a schedule of events for tourist attractions in our area
- Small chocolates, left on their pillows

Though we can't always make all these provisions, we try to arrange for as many as possible.

Occasionally, if we're celebrating a special event such as the guest's birthday, or if we sense the guest needs some extra affirmation, we provide a surpise breakfast in bed with the "You Are Special" dishes (see chapter 45).

Some families keep a guest preference book, indexing the pages of a notebook in alphabetical order to record guests' names. When someone visits, they make a note of any special likes or dislikes the person has in areas such as food, entertainment, sleeping accommodations, special health needs, or whatever. When guests return, the host family refers to the notebook to plan the visit.

When it's time to send our guests back home, we pack them some provisions for the road. Then we hold hands in a circle and pray for their safety as they travel.

Through all these strategies, we try to make guests feel like royalty when they stay with us. A tradition of hospitality is one of the best ways we know to extend the warmth and love of our home to people beyond our family.

51 ■ Welcome New Neighbors

There was a time when folks moving into a new area could count on their neighbors to help them get established—even if that meant lending a hand to build a new home. Today, however, many families consider themselves lucky just to know the names of a family or two on the block.

In this situation as in others, the old saying holds true: you have to *be* a friend to *have* a friend. The surest way to begin building a relationship with another family on your street is to reach out with a helping hand when they need it most: on the day they move in!

Moving Day Customs We try to make contact with new neighbors as soon as possible, preferably with home-baked goodies in hand. Unless we're busy with other responsibilities, we offer assistance with unloading, unpacking, or other moving chores. It's easy to break the ice with someone when the two of you are squeezing through a door on either end of a sofa.

That kind of welcome to the neighborhood has always resulted in a warm acquaintance at the very least, and sometimes an enduring friendship has blossomed. Of course, since we've moved many times ourselves, we've often been on the receiving end of neighborly kindness as well. All in all, God has given us wonderful neighbors in every place we've lived—and our moving day experiences with them were usually the occasion when we found out just how wonderful they were.

A Neighborhood Guide   For a welcome-to-the-neighborhood tradition that will help your new friends for weeks to come, create for them a personalized guide to your area. Here's how:

Pick up a free map of your area from the local chamber of commerce, tourist information center, or automobile association. Use the map as a basis for a resource directory of businesses, professional offices, and public services close to your neighborhood. On a separate sheet, make a list of

- the businesses you've patronized and found satisfactory, especially the essentials such as supermarkets, banks, and department stores.

- your doctors, dentist, pharmacist, and veterinarian (add the notation that your name can be used as a referral).

- the nearest post office, library, hospital, schools, and community college.

- local government administration buildings.

- playgrounds, parks, and other recreational sites.

- malls and major shopping centers.

Number the places you've identified, and then write those numbers in the corresponding locations on the map in a bright color.

Add information such as the phone numbers of the electric company and gas company, the days for garbage pickup, and the time and place of the neighborhood school bus stop. If you enjoy a particular annual event in your area such as a seasonal festival, craft fair, or parade, note that as well. List your own name and phone number just in case you've missed something and your new neighbor has a question. Finally, make a photocopy of your guide before you present it. You'll be saving yourself some work when the next new neighbor moves in!

52 ■ Remember These Guidelines for Making It Work

You now have an abundance of ideas to choose from as you seek to weave new traditions into the fabric of your family life. Drawing from the suggestions in this book, as well as from the sources noted in chapter 2, you can cultivate customs that affirm your cherished values, honor your family members, and celebrate your life together.

Things to Remember As you consider which of all these traditions will be best suited to your home, keep in mind a few important guidelines to help you make the wisest choices:

Simple customs are best. Elaborate or expensive rituals may be difficult to maintain. Make sure that the burden of preparation doesn't fall on one person. Consistency is the key, not complexity.

The kernels of corn our family uses at the Thanksgiving meal, for example, work well in part because they require so little time and money to prepare. On the other hand, other traditions we once observed—such as stringing popcorn and cranberries for the Christmas tree every year— eventually lapsed because they took too much time and effort.

Prepare for family traditions well ahead of time— weeks or even months if necessary. Preparation builds anticipation, which is also part of the fun. Avoid canceling or changing plans on the spur of the moment.

Choose and maintain traditions that focus on values and relationships, rather than on costly gifts or activities. For example, a homemade valentine crafted especially for your spouse every year may mean a great deal more than an annual (and overpriced) bouquet of roses.

Make sure every family member is included in the planning, preparation, and observance of every tradition. Also make sure that the customs you establish appeal to old and young alike. The benefit of family unity and closeness will be lost if someone is left out. Waiting to decorate the Christmas tree until everyone has a free evening may mean waiting later than you'd prefer, but if it's a special family custom, the waiting will be worth the joy of having everyone take part.

Include a few customs that turn your family outward. Many Jewish families, for example, invite a stranger to their table for the Passover meal—an ancient tradition reflecting the biblical command for God's people to remember their exile in Egypt by caring for the stranger in their midst (see Ex. 23:9).

Don't be pressured or rigid about observing traditions.   If you have to enforce a tradition, you take the fun out of it. When an idea doesn't work, try a different one.

Look for traditions that are tied to recurring events. Weekly, monthly, seasonal, or annual events keep the observances alive naturally.

Use family traditions to teach your children.   Call attention to the significance of an occasion. This is the biblical pattern: Moses told the Israelites that when their children asked why the Passover was kept, the parents were to discuss with the young ones the tradition's special meaning (see Deut. 6:20–25).

What better time to tell our children about God's love for the world than on Christmas Eve, or to affirm His power than on Easter morning? And a wedding anniversary is the perfect occasion to talk with teens about romance and marriage.

With these guidelines in mind, you should be able to create and maintain a beautiful heritage of family traditions unique to your home. The benefits of that heritage are immediate and they last a lifetime, so don't wait—today is the day to get started.